FORMATION IN THE LOVE OF TRUTH:
Principles of Orthodox Education

Christ Teaching in the Temple

Visoki Dečani Monastery, Serbia - 14th century

FORMATION IN THE LOVE OF TRUTH:

Principles of Orthodox Education

By Archpriest Peter Heers

Uncut Mountain Press
EDUCATION

FORMATION IN THE LOVE OF TRUTH
Principles of Orthodox Education
© 2024
Uncut Mountain Press Education
An imprint of Uncut Mountain Press

All rights reserved under International and Pan-American Copyright Conventions.

uncutmountainpress.com

Interior images are from Uncut Mountain Supply or in the public domain unless otherwise referenced.

Scriptural quotations are primarily taken from the King James Version. The translator has emended some quotations to better reflect the original Greek text.

Archpriest Peter Alban Heers, 1971–

Formation in the Love of Truth: Principles of Orthodox Education.—1st Ed.

ISBN: 978-1-63941-063-7

I. Eastern Orthodox Theology
II. Orthodox Christian Education

"But the natural man receiveth not the things of the Spirit of God: for they are foolishness unto him: neither can he know them, because they are spiritually discerned. But he that is spiritual judgeth all things, yet he himself is judged of no man. For who hath known the mind of the Lord, that he may instruct him? But we have the mind of Christ."

I Corinthians 2:14–16 KJV

"We are heading again to the secret schools.... The priest, or whoever was educated in the community, in the villages, would teach the children using the liturgical books of the Church. The great educator and apostle to Greece, Saint Kosmas Aitolos, said famously... 'you must educate your children, open up schools if possible, but educate your children.'....This is why we have to understand that our role is not to have great ideas for our children's educational future, but to be focused on the preservation of the faith.... this is the end goal of their education: to serve their salvation and to serve the Church."

From the lecture "Have Faith"

CONTENTS

Publisher's Note 13

CHAPTER I: Have Faith: Examining Homeschooling and Compulsory State Education 17

    Introductory Remarks 17
        At Stake is Not Simply Education,
            But the faithfulness of Our Children to Christ 17
        Fr. Peter's Homeschooling Experience in Greece 18
        Presentation Overview 20
    I. **Compulsory State Schooling Compared to Homeschooling** 22
        Mistaken Views and the Truth Concerning
            Homeschooling 22
        The Innovation is Not Homeschooling;
            It is Collective and Obligatory State Education 24
        Ways to Put Homeschooling Into Practice 25
        What do the Test Results Reveal 27
    II. **Homeschooling Throughout the World** 29
        Homeschool Laws by State 32
    III. **History of Compulsory Education** 33
        Compulsory Education is Not About Education;
            it is About Control 33
        Compulsory Education Began with the Reformation;
            Prussia First to Impose Mandate 34
        Aim is to Create Obedient Citizens Who Think
            Identically 35
        Compulsory Education Intended to Satisfy
            the Needs of the Society/State 36

Totalitarian Governments Required Compulsory Education Through Secondary Education, Banned Homeschooling 37
Harsh Repression of Homeschooling by Several European Governments 38
United Nations Convention on the Rights of a Child Document Impinges on Parents' Freedom to Homeschool 40
General State Education is About the Interest of the State, Not the Children or the Parents 41

IV. **Homeschooling: Not an Option, but a Necessity** **42**
Homeschooling is About "Having Faith"; the Survival of Our Christian Identity and the Church 42
We Homeschool to Remain Faithful to Christ; Public Schools Do Not Equal Education 44
Homeschooling Avoids Internet Addiction 46
Christians Should Plan a Christian Education Future for Their Children Which Forms Their Souls 47
Control by the State is Our Future 48
The History and Return of the Secret Schools; Preservation of the Faith 48
Two Kinds of Faith 49

Question & Answer Session from "Have Faith: Examining Homeschooling and Compulsory State Education" **53**

Question 1: It seems like there is a pattern already established by the Church for spiritually and educationally forming our children. Could we, and why do we not, have a pure Orthodox curriculum that could be followed by parents, of course along with the support of a spiritual father? **53**

Question 2: Father Seraphim Rose advocated the use of western music and literature for the cultivation of the soul. We are told of him and of other spiritual fathers having novices read Dickens and Dostoevsky in order to develop normal feelings and warmth of the heart. Would you consider this a proper use of western literature? **54**

Question 3: Please clarify what you include in the category of pagan knowledge, and worldly knowledge. Are you speaking about literature only, or other subjects like logic, rhetoric, etc.? Would education of the theologians and orators, and persuasive speaking, logic, etc., be beneficial to our kids in terms of understanding truth and combating fallacy in the world? 56

Question 4: Could you talk a little bit about why St. Basil, being raised in a pious Christian family, went off unbaptized to study pagan wisdom? 56

Question 5: What is the value, if any, of studying ancient, or current philosophy at the upper school or college level? 57

Question 6: How would you define the Greek word "παιδεία" (*paideia*)? What components of development does it encompass? Does it encompass spiritual formation? Is there any better word in Greek to describe the education and formation of a child? 58

Question 7: What should be the classical language of choice? Why are most Orthodox classical educators in America pushing Latin over Greek? What are the advantages of having Orthodox children learn Greek over Latin? 59

Question 8: I have heard the words "heart," "*nous*," "eye of the soul," and today "spirit" used in close association. Are these terms synonymous? If distinct, how are they different? Is the term "*phronema*" distinct from the terms above? How does the phrase "mind of Christ" relate to these other terms? 60

Question 9: My son is thinking about going into psychology. What are your thoughts on how to choose a school for that field of study, and what are your recommendations for how to navigate through the messed-up thought in that field? 62

Question 10: I have just begun the book *Orthodox Psychotherapy*. Is that a different vein from what we are discussing here regarding Orthodox psychologists?..................................... 65

Question 11: How does one remove harmful literature from the home without causing the children to turn away from God in rebellion? How do I avoid the introduction of what I think is not useful to my younger children by older siblings?... 66

Question 12: Does Christian fantasy, like Tolkien and C.S. Lewis, fall into the same category as mythology,

in terms of what you described in your talk
earlier today? **68**

Question 13: What do you feel would be an appropriate
age to begin reading the Scriptures to children?
My oldest is nine but sometimes when I try to read
to them, it does not go how I hope. **70**

Question 14: Do you find it helpful to have a dedicated
place for your children to do homeschooling, or is
the kitchen table fine? **70**

Question 15: At what age should we start reading to
them the Lives of the Saints? **71**

Question 16: My personal reading of the Lives of the Saints
has come only from the big books that you buy of an
individual saint, but are you talking about something
that is concise for each saint? **72**

Question 17: There was a time in my life when I tried to
completely cut off all non-Orthodox things and it
drove me a little bit crazy because I was constantly
questioning, "Is that Orthodox? Is it not Orthodox?
Who is the author?" and I feel like I was being a little
too paranoid. So, I am trying to understand:
Is it prescriptive? Or is it not a set rule? **73**

Question 18: At what age do you recommend that
children start confessing? **77**

Question 19: We are very strict about what we let our kids
watch. We do not let them watch very many of the
Disney movies. They have seen very few movies that are
rated above PG. Some G movies we do not let them see
because some of those cartoons are just terrible.
How do I encourage them so that they do not feel
bitter or resentful? How do I help them avoid feeling
like they are missing out on something? **80**

CHAPTER II: Seeking Truth:
Forming Children in the Love of Truth **87**

Of What the Love of Truth Consists and
Why it is Necessary for Us to Impart it **88**

Truth is Manifested to Us in Two Different Ways;
On a Vertical Plane and on a Horizontal Plane **92**

We Love Truth as Christ Himself When We Live
in Him and Acquire His Mind **93**

The Mind of Christ is not the Rational Mind............................ **96**
The Mind of Christ is Speaking and
  Witnessing to the Truth **98**

**CHAPTER III: On the Patristic and
"Post-Patristic" View of Education
and Salvation** **105**
  The Meaning of the "Post-Patristic" View and
    How it Has Affected Homeschooling **106**
  The Fathers of the Church and Classical Education **110**
    A. Two Types of Wisdom **111**
    B. St. Basil the Great and His Example **114**
  The Diachronic Witness of the Fathers on the
    Superiority of Christian Wisdom **117**
  Coming to the Knowledge (ἐπίγνωσης) of the Truth **119**
  The Work of Initiating Our Children into the Mystery **122**
  The Use of θύραθεν Philosophy in
    Christian Education Today **124**

**CHAPTER IV: The Central Place
of the Orthodox Academy in the
Church's Resistance to Secularism** **131**
  Theory **135**
  Practice **146**

**Question and Answer Session from "The
Central Place of the Orthodox Academy in
the Church's Resistance to Secularism"**........................... **157**
  Question 1: Concerning "teaching to the exam"
    and the SAT. **157**
  Question 2: Concerning how texts are to be read
    and analyzed. **159**
  Question 3: Concerning continuing education
    then and now. **160**
  Question 4: Concerning the world forcing its needs
    upon the school's development. **161**
  Question 5: Concerning how the parents and adults
    in the school effectively work towards its future................. **163**

Question 6: Concerning how the school handles its
existence in a foreign community and its struggle
against urbanization. **167**

Question 7: Concerning the relationship of the school
with parishes. **172**

Question 8: Concerning languages. **173**

Question 9: Concerning the position of the
non-Orthodox. **174**

Question 10: Concerning safeguards against
error in teaching. **176**

About the Author **179**

Christ in the Synagogue of Nazareth

PUBLISHER'S NOTE

In the West, we are inheritors of a robust educational tradition. In the nineteenth and twentieth centuries, however, we, the citizens of Western society, saw this tradition transformed into a mechanism of totalitarian political control through compulsory state education. All major Western nations, regardless of whether they were of fascist, communist, liberal, or even monarchical constitution, succumbed to this distorted view on education. This fraudulent educational system dominates our society to this day.

As Orthodox Christians living in the West in this situation, we have the responsibility not only to learn the place of education in relation to our Faith and Holy Tradition but also to realize the progressive corruption of education since the time when the West lost its grace due to heresy and schism. With these lectures, given in 2018 and 2019, Archpriest Peter Heers (D. Th.) provides Orthodox Christians with the principles which ought to govern our education as the acquisition of knowledge and growth in virtue, as explicated in the Holy Scriptures and among the Holy Fathers. Fr. Peter shares his experience and observations to inform all Orthodox Christian educators (at home or in parish schools) of the work still needed for our Church's investment, through our children, in the future.

In these four lectures, we learn about the history of compulsory state education, the different methods by which our souls acquire knowledge and understand the truth, how the Holy Fathers understood the distinction between spiritual wisdom and philosophical knowledge, the theory and practice of how this vision may be seen and applied in the specific realm of education, and over two dozen questions and answers which serve to complete one's understanding of the principles presented in these lectures. Whether one chooses to homeschool, do a homeschool co-op, or participate in a private Orthodox school, Uncut Mountain Press believes any of these environments will benefit from this book and the principles found herein.

To Kryfo Scholio (*The Secret School*).

Nikolaos Gyzis, Oil on Canvas

Saint Basil the Great

CHAPTER I

Have Faith: Examining Homeschooling & Compulsory State Education

Lecture delivered at the
Orthodox Homeschool Conference: "Have Faith"
April 19-22, 2018
St. Nicholas Ranch, Dunlap, CA

INTRODUCTORY REMARKS

At Stake is Not Simply Education, But the Faithfulness of Our Children to Christ

It is a great joy and blessing for me to be here, back in California, as Fr. Paul said. I grew up in the East Bay, from age ten to nineteen—before I went away to college. And I spent my formative three or four years before I went to Greece in this area, going to St. John, the relics, and Platina, and many other places. So, it is a joy to be back. Actually, in this place right here, I met Elder Ephraim for the first time, twenty-four years ago. So this brings back a lot of memories.

I want to thank the director of the conference for inviting me. She has done a tremendous job. Thank you very much, Christine, for inviting me and allowing me to be here and to speak to you. Fr. Noah as well, who is an old friend on the East Coast and also involved.

My topic today is "Have Faith," and the directions that I received from the director of the conference, regarding the topic was, "This needs to be motivational. We need to give people courage in this struggle for home education, and not just for educating, but actually imparting the faith." I think this is one of the main reasons why we are all here and why we are all believers in homeschooling and struggling to continue, because we understand what is at stake is not simply the education of our children, but the faithfulness of our children to Christ.

This is why today I am going to focus a little bit—as a jumping off point—on homeschooling in relation to state compulsory schooling and history. I think it is important for us to see the big picture. We start out homeschooling, we are looking at our small children, and we look at the various things we need to do to impart to them the basics, and a lot of us are uneasy. Are we really capable? Can we really do this? But if we step back and see the larger picture, I think it is very encouraging. It is also very frightening, when we see the history of compulsory schooling. But it is also encouraging, because we see that homeschooling is so very necessary, not just for ourselves, but for the Church and for the survival of the Church as we go forward.

Fr. Peter's Homeschooling Experience in Greece

I started out my homeschooling in Greece about eighteen years ago, and you might not know, but in Greece, it is actually illegal to homeschool. It is not allowed. You have to send your children to the state school. It is kind of ironic that here we are in California and you are free to homeschool, but in Greece you are not. So, as an American citizen, I did it anyway. I was an illegal homeschooler for my entire eighteen years in Greece.

I want to tell you a little story about what I encountered with the Greek state schooling system, because I think it is encouraging, in that it shows that God is above all and encourages us in everything we do. About two years into homeschooling, I was in the village, up in the mountains outside Thessaloniki, where we lived (a very small village). Eventually someone told the school down in the next city: "You know, Fr. Peter, who is the priest of the village, is not sending his kids to school. What is going on?" Those school officials called us in and they said, "You need to be sending your kids to school." We said, "Well, actually, no we do not. I am an American citizen, and in America this is the kind of education system that we have, and our children are enrolled there, online." We were enrolled with St. John of Shanghai and San Francisco Academy and we called it "distance learning." We presented them the paperwork, and they did not really know what to make of it. Probably because in Greece there are about five or ten people who homeschool, and they are probably all foreigners. In any case, the school official said, "I have to submit the paperwork to the state because this is a requirement. You have to send your kids to school." He then tried to convince us why it is so important to send our kids to school.

You might say, "Well, why, Fr. Peter, did you feel it is so necessary?" being in Greece compared to California. You will see, after I present about compulsory state education, why I think it is necessary. Comparatively, fifteen, eighteen years ago things were much better—and probably much better than California in terms of the kind of influences they were bringing into the school system. However, it goes beyond only the threats and moral problems in the school. It goes to the whole heart of what it means to raise a child, how to raise a child, how that child is going to react to you, and when he or she should start learning, and when he or she should start leaving the house and being far from the mother and father. There is a lot more to homeschooling than just the education. It is much more involved. Compulsory state education is actually much more diabolical than it looks, when you understand the history.

Back to the story... we stood our ground and he sent the papers to the state of Greece, the department of education for the state of Greece. We never heard from them. We did our education for the next fifteen years in Greece for all of our children. I still do not know what happened. My guess is they simply said, "Why bother with the crazy priest up in the mountains from America?"

Later, we learned that there were more Greeks becoming interested in homeschooling in Greece. We learned that other people too, in Greece, had fought to have control over the education of their children, and they had been successful. Some had sent their children abroad, and others had done school via the internet. Increasingly, what has happened in Greece since that time—just to share something that I am sure most of you do not know—has been the introduction of transgenderism, homosexuality, and teaching sexual education to very young children. Many other things have been introduced into the schools in Greece, with the result that there have been more and more people who are interested in homeschooling in Greece.

Presentation Overview

So, let me begin by going through this presentation on homeschooling and state compulsory education. Then we will stop and talk about this whole question of faith and give you some examples. Initially, this will be a little bit repetitive if you have already been homeschooling. Once we get to the compulsory state education history, however, hopefully that will be interesting and new for all of you. What I am going to look at in this short presentation is:

I. Compulsory State Schooling Compared to Homeschooling
II. Homeschooling Around the World Today
III. A History of Compulsory State Education
IV. Homeschooling: Not an Option, but a Necessity

I. Compulsory State Schooling Compared to Homeschooling

Mistaken Views & the Truth Concerning Homeschooling

Many times people say, "Well, you know, homeschooling is so restrictive. The child is not allowed to socialize." In Greece especially, I heard that line continually. "You have to socialize your children." "You have to become a part of society." Now, of course, who is not for good socialization and learning all the skills of the social life? The question is, what kind of socialization? What are they learning? As Orthodox Christians, first and foremost, we want to impart to our children the path of the commandments, to initiate them into the mystery of Christ, to have in their life examples of virtue; and so socialization for its own sake is not good. Socialization so that they might become children of God and brothers and sisters in Christ is absolutely what we all want.

And in the popular mind, which is not looking at it from the Orthodox Christian's perspective, the myth is that to be a homeschooler, your children are going to be isolated and afraid. The reality is just the opposite, if you are doing your homework as a homeschooler. Of course, it is all dependent on the grace of God and our struggle. The reality is that public schooling is impersonal at the end of the day, and it is not going to deal with the needs of each child. It is not personal or one-to-one, and it is not going at the pace that the child needs.

I was just in New York, talking to one of my fellow professors who had to stop homeschooling. She was pregnant and gave birth, and she had to send her child to a private school for about 6 months. She said after her daughter was being homeschooled and after she was being tutored (by what I think was a Montessori-type education), she was extremely bored and restless in school. This is one of the side-effects. When the child is really engaged early on and learns to love learning, and love discovery, and love the interaction on a personal level, then if they go to school, they are very restless, and then bad things start to happen. Very bright children usually have this problem. They have so much energy, and so much ability to learn, that if you are not continually feeding them, they get involved in things that are not profitable. So this is the myth, that we are very restrictive in homeschooling and that it is deficient, when in reality it is just the opposite.

There are many mistaken views concerning homeschooling on account of ignorance, lack of experience, fear of not having the safety of the education system—even though this has failed!—and because of the parent's psychological insecurity. I know I am speaking to the choir here, but the truth is that homeschooling has at least six advantages:

1. It unites families.
2. It gives students opportunities to excel.
3. It widens horizons.
4. It protects innocence, which is something the world is not going to tell you that you need to do. The world is not going to come and say, "the purity of the soul of your child is most important." No one from the state school or from society is going to say that, and yet that is one of the most important things you can do as a parent: protect them from defilement in images and in concepts. That is not going to happen in a social setting in contemporary schools.

5. It deepens faith and morality. One of the reasons why it is going to do that is because the child is going to see much more of his or her parents living out the faith on a daily basis. One of the great blessings we had in Greece was that my children were constantly with me on feast days and we were going to church, or we were going to pilgrimages; the restriction that school would have given to us was not present. So as a family, but also in terms of the faith, they had many more opportunities to grow.

6. It also promotes healthy children. This is for a variety of reasons, because usually children are getting sick in school, and not just physically, but also spiritually.

The Innovation is Not Homeschooling; It is Collective and Obligatory State Education

One of the other myths is that homeschooling is a great innovation and that this is something that started in the 20th century. In fact, homeschooling has existed ever since there have been parents. It is the norm, and the innovation is compulsory state education.

From the time of the fourth century, the Church Fathers' elementary education—ages seven to fourteen—was done exclusively at home. The great St. Basil, who everybody refers to in terms of classical education and the Christian understanding of it, when do you think he went to school? He was about fifteen years old when he actually left the house and went to school. Secondary education was from about age fourteen to fifteen on.

So this idea that children need to leave at age five—and now it is even three or four to go to a babysitter—is the exception, it is the innovation. And it is very dangerous and very problematic for the development of the child to leave his mother and father so early. Kindergarten and day care were entirely unknown during ancient times; the majority of the saints were homeschooled. If you look at the Lives of the Saints and you pay attention, you will see that the idea of state school did not exist. Education was done on a tutoring basis, and the norm was much later than it is today.

St. Basil the Great himself supported the personalization of instruction as something necessary. In fact, this personalization was on the level of individuals, not of groups of students. So when they talk about "schools," in the first millennium at least, they did not mean universities like we see them today, with massive amounts of people. They meant a teacher or two and a few students; that was the "school" in a lot of places. Very few people were educated at the level that we tend to think. We think that back in ancient times people were educated. Well, very few of them were educated compared to the numbers who are today. Today we have a massive increase in the mass education of many people, but the level of education generally has declined immensely.

When do you think that compulsory state education began? How many years ago? Right at the beginning of the nineteenth century. So it is 200 years old. It slowly developed. Only in the twentieth century do we see the kind of state education that exists today.

Ways to Put Homeschooling into Practice

You already know how to do this, how to put it into practice. This was a presentation that I originally gave to clergy in Greece, because the people (clergy at a clergy conference) were asking me, "What is this homeschooling that you are doing?" I presented it to them, and so some of this is more applicable to people who are totally new to homeschooling.

But there are a wide variety of things that people can do in terms of homeschooling in North America, in terms of interaction with other homeschoolers. Of course, the Orthodox community is not that big; one needs to have discernment on what kind of interaction you are going to have with non-Orthodox homeschoolers, but there are plenty of things available in most communities today, so you can take advantage of that. The flexibility of homeschooling allows for homeschoolers a great spectrum of choices concerning the method and curriculum.

Orthodox homeschooling in North America has groups of "homeschoolers" under the auspices of the monasteries. Parish schools also exist that serve as "umbrella schools" for homeschooling. We sometimes see cooperation between Orthodox families for home learning (i.e., alternating instruction of small groups of children by parents). With homeschooling, there are also great educational possibilities that open up. These include public libraries, museums, Church schools, associations (with various activities for children, parks, and other social activities), online education, early entry into university classes, and homeschooling co-ops.

A growing number of resources are available too in North America. We have homeschooling friendly environments (often near the monasteries), others in the parish (especially when the clergy are supportive of homeschooling), homeschooling conferences, Orthodox educational websites and blogs, sometimes even parish schools. So these are means and ways of putting homeschooling into practice, especially as we are seeing in North America. However, my concern is more about the history of compulsory state education.

What Do the Test Results Reveal?

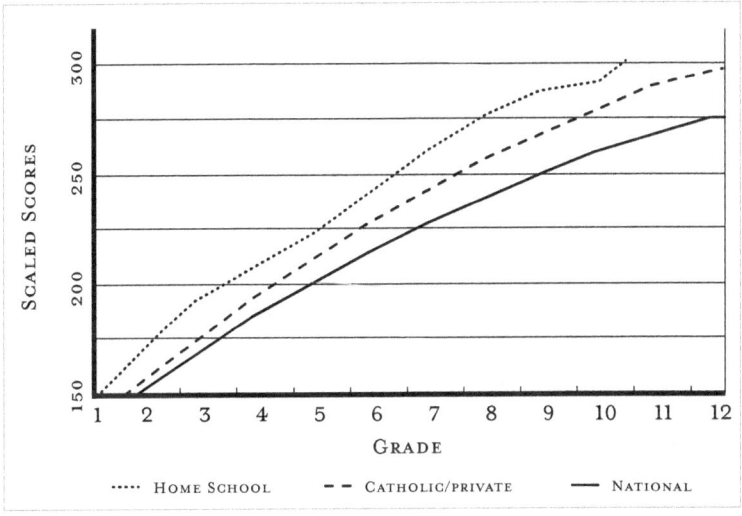

1998 Scholastic Achievement Comparison - Homeschool vs Catholic/Private School[1]

---

[1] Lawrence M. Rudner, "Scholastic Achievement and Demographic Characteristics of Home School Students in 1998," accessed April 29, 2024, https://eric.ed.gov/?id=ED424309

1998 Testing Comparison - Homeschool vs National Norm[2]

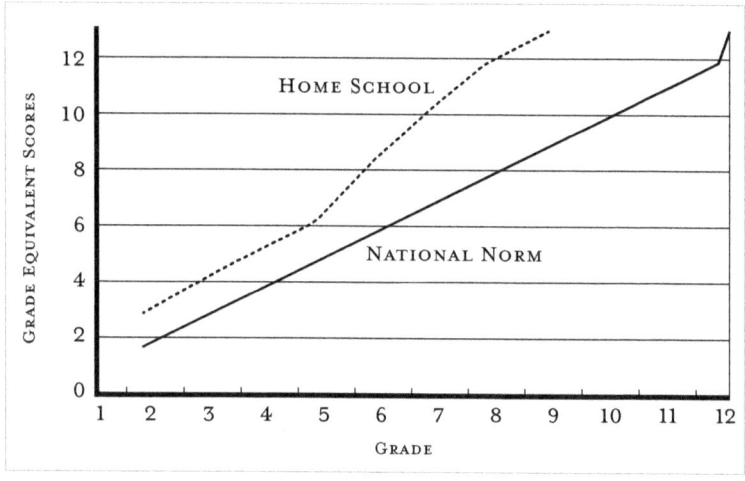

So these are some of the things that I found a few years ago which showed that actually (as you probably already know) homeschoolers did better on tests and academics. This is the main point that people bring up, especially in Europe, "Well, homeschoolers really academically are not going to flourish," when in fact they flourish and in the preponderance cases they do better than most students in the public schools.

---

2   Ibid.

II. Homeschooling Throughout the World

Homeschooling: Is it Legal?[3]

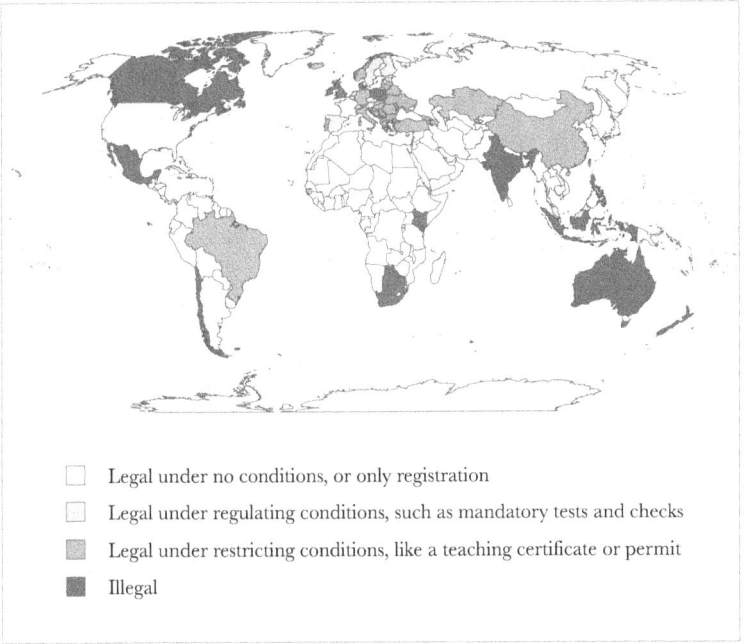

- ☐ Legal under no conditions, or only registration
- ☐ Legal under regulating conditions, such as mandatory tests and checks
- ▨ Legal under restricting conditions, like a teaching certificate or permit
- ▪ Illegal

(*For the United States and Switzerland legal status varies by state, color by most occurring)

I do not know if you have seen this, but this is an example of more and more countries allowing homeschooling at different levels of legality. There are a few countries without presuppositions at all, not many. In some parts of the world, especially in eastern Europe, in a lot of places, it is illegal to homeschool, but that is changing every day.

In Europe there are thirty countries in which it is legal to homeschool, although the homeschooling movements are

---

3   "Homeschooling: Is it Legal?", accessed April 29, 2024, https://homeschooling.fandom.com/wiki/Is_it_legal%3F

pretty small in most of those countries.[4] There are six countries in which it is illegal,[5] with Germany being the most well-known and repressive. In Sweden, while it is actually, technically legal, there is a lot of repression.

Orthodox countries that do not allow homeschooling are Bulgaria, Greece, and Romania. It is understandable in some ways why an Orthodox country would not be open to homeschooling as much as the western countries, because there would not have been the need historically. The rationale would be harder to sell in a homogeneous society like Greece, so historically there are reasons why people would frown on homeschooling in Greece. With the rise of many minorities and the decline of Orthodox education in the state schools, though, it makes a lot more sense to do homeschooling in Orthodox countries as we go forward. Russia and the Ukraine, of the Orthodox countries, are the ones where it is legal.

England and France are leaders of homeschooling in Europe and have thousands of homeschoolers. However, it is always a tenuous relationship. Although it grows slowly in England, it has not really established itself, and there is always pressure, and there are always laws.[6] There is always a struggle in these countries, even though it is legal to homeschool. Between 20,0000 and 100,000 children home-

---

4   Austria, Andorra, Belgium, Belarus, Czech Republic, Denmark, Estonia, Finland, France, Hungary, Iceland, Ireland, Italy, Latvia, Lichtenstein, Luxemburg, Lithuania, Monaco, Moldova, Norway, Poland, Portugal, San Marino, Sweden, Switzerland, Slovenia, Spain, United Kingdom, Russia, and the Ukraine.

5   Germany, Slovakia, Bulgaria, Romania, Holland, and Greece (the status of homeschooling in the former Yugoslav countries and in Albania is unclear).

6   As of March 2024, a proposed law in the UK seeks to create a homeschooling registry.

school in the United Kingdom. There were eight thousand independent homeschoolers, as of a couple of years ago, in France, with a further two thousand student cooperating with the public schools.

In the United Kingdom, homeschooling's legal status is by the Education Act of 1944, revised in 1996. The Education Act of 1996 (Section 7) mentions "…[E]fficient full-time education suitable (a) to his age, ability and aptitude, and (b) to any special educational needs he may have, either by regular attendance at school or otherwise." Under cover of the phrase "or otherwise," families homeschool legally. It is not a presupposition that the authorities be informed that someone homeschools, unless the student was formerly enrolled in the school system.

In France, homeschooling is legal. Certain families are obligated to undergo some inspection of their level in relation to the correlating level of public schools, but many families have politely refused this presupposition disputing the law. The law is unclear and disputable.

Homeschool Laws by State[7]

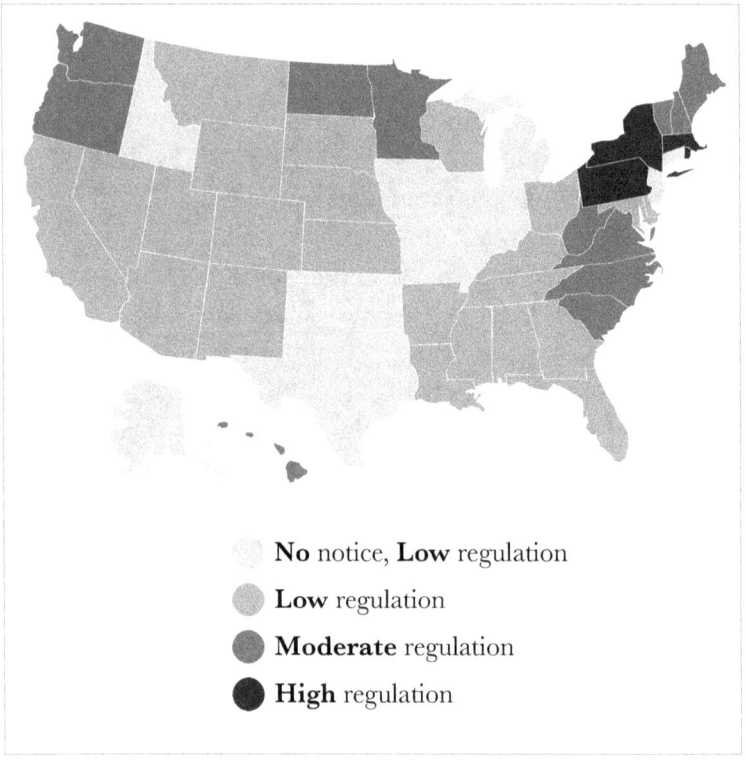

In the United States, homeschooling is legal, but with varying degrees of strictness by state. Homeschooling is the most rapidly developing form of education in the United States. The "Home School Legal Defense Association,"[8] is an organization that provides excellent legal support and information regarding homeschooling in the United States.

---

7 "Homeschool Laws by State," Home School Legal Defense Association, accessed April 29, 2024, https://hslda.org/legal

8 Home School Legal Defense Association - https://hslda.org

III. HISTORY OF COMPULSORY EDUCATION

Compulsory Education is Not About Education; it is About Control

Here is where we get to the history of compulsory school. And I want to go slow here and talk a little about the history because it is very instructive. The spirit behind compulsory state schooling is not about school and not about education at all. It is about control. State education is the government's war against parents to control the mind of the children. Compulsory state education is coercion of the population; that is its history. Compulsory state education has always been about control. There is an ideology behind it that pushes it, which is the controlling of the society, and also coercing the society in a certain direction. This becomes clear when we actually see the history of compulsory state education.

So, what do we mean by the phrase "compulsory state education"? Compulsory state education is not the citizen's right to access education, but rather it is the state's right to compel parents to send their children to public school. That is the proper understanding. Parents, when they are in charge—which the United States recognizes—can choose many ways to educate their children. But when it is compulsory state education, those choices are no longer available to parents. So the correct stance should be to provide the citizen with free access to education through various means, public and private. One researcher said that "if we look into the history of the drive for public schooling and compulsory attendance in this and other countries, we find at the root not so much misguided altruism as a conscious scheme to coerce the mass of the population into a mould desired by the Establishment..."⁹ Compulsory state education began in Prussia; and when it began, this compulsory approach was behind it.

Compulsory Education Began with the Reformation; Prussia First to Impose Mandate

What are the roots of compulsory education? Well, they start with the Protestant Reformation, especially Luther and Calvin. This is not an accident. This modern movement on behalf of compulsory state education is the direct fruit of the Reformation. The Reformation was the force behind the introduction of compulsory education in Germany in the sixteenth century. The Reformers, particularly Martin Luther, wanted to have parents conform to the state system. He devised a school plan, which was later applied in Germany. He considered schools as a means of (εμποτισμού) implanting ideas into the whole population. He was unrelenting that the state should employ supreme strictness against those citizens who would not become Lutheran. This was the age in Europe where people were persecuted for not following the state religion, including many Protestants who were persecuted by other Protestants, and his views left an indelible mark on Germany, which to this day imposes a totalitarian approach to education.

Similarly, Protestant reformer John Calvin was a senior pastor in Geneva (1536 to 1564) and he also introduced compulsory education when he was head of his religious state. He wanted schools to serve the spread of Calvinism. No liberty or right was to supplant the state's power. He considered the support of Calvinism to be the end and purpose of the state. As Calvinists spread to France and

---

9   Murray N. Rothbard, *For a New Liberty*, 2ⁿᵈ ed. (Auburn, AL: Ludwig von Mises Institute, 2006), pp. 148-149.

Scotland, compulsory education spread with them to these other states. And English Puritans influenced by Calvin's ideas brought compulsory education to New England. However, Prussia was the most authoritarian state in Europe and first to enforce the compulsory education system. The king of Prussia was the first one to really impose this on a statewide basis. This was Frederick William I (1688–1740). He was known as the Soldier King for his monarchist authoritarianism. He increased the Prussian army, created a centralizing bureaucracy, imposed limitations on trade, and inaugurated the Prussian compulsory school system which was the first national system in Europe. Califon Hayes states: "He treated his kingdom as a schoolroom, and like a zealous schoolmaster, flogged his naughty subjects unmercifully."[10] The whole point was to create the school system so that he could have people in the mechanism of the state.

Aim is to Create Obedient Citizens Who Think Identically

The philosopher Johann Fichte, in his "Address to the German People"(1807-1808), was promoting the state as an instrument of societal progress, a part of which was compulsory education. The aims of the utopian system, which began in 1819, were obedient soldiers, servile workers, docile civil servants, compliant administrative assistants, and citizens who think identically concerning the major issues. His aim was not to develop understanding, but to socialize the children in obedience and submission.

So socialization was always at the heart of compulsory state education. When people say, "You need to be in the

---

10   Murray N. Rothbard, "Compulsory Schooling in Europe" in *Free and Compulsory Education*, (Auburn, AL: Ludwig Von Mises Institute, 1999), p. 25.

state schools because you need to be socialized," they are right. That is what the main point of state education is. It is not about education. Of course, there are people there who really want education in spite of the system, and there are people who are getting educated in spite of the system, but we are talking about how it began and why it began politically.

Compulsory Education Intended to Satisfy the Needs of the Society/State

Intentionally (in the beginning), this first example of state education, only 8% of the children were given secondary education (*Real Schulen*). Secondary education was not open to all the students. Ninety-two percent of the children were educated at the elementary level only (*Volksschule*)— intentionally left there—because the idea was not to bring everyone up to a grand level of Renaissance erudition; the point was to create a working force that could serve the new and rising power of the state, and industrialization.

Country	Year	Children enrolled in 1870 (%)
Prussia	1763	67
Denmark	1814	58
Greece	1834	20
Sweden	1842	71
Portugal	1844	13
Norway	1848	61
USA	1852–1918	72
Italy	1877	29
UK	1880	49
France	1882	75

Introduction of Laws Requiring Compulsory Education

This is a list of when compulsory education was introduced in these countries. Notice Greece. In 1834, when Greece had adopted compulsory state education, it was just after the Revolution. So it was very young (as a nation-state) and it was free from the Turks, but immediately compulsory education was forced on Greece by Otto, the new king who was brought from Germany into Greek government. He brought with him the German system of education and limited—almost got rid of—the reading of the holy books (liturgical, etc.) in grade school.

Notice America. Compulsory education was slowly codified in the United States from 1852 to 1918. Yet by 1870, compulsory education reached 72%, one of the highest of all the countries. It very quickly rose in America, thanks to people like John Dewey, and centralization, and the closing of the one-room schoolhouses in the last part of the nineteenth century. That was seen as especially necessary in America because we had such a divergent population and they wanted to form a common mind and society. So again in America, we see that the main thrust here is not education per se, but socialization, and the needs of the society or the state.

Totalitarian Governments Required Compulsory Education Through Secondary Education, Banned Homeschooling

So, the nineteenth century saw the slow rise of compulsory education, but that was still only to the third, fourth, fifth, at the most sixth grade. It was not until the totalitarian governments in the twentieth century that you had this very quick increase to eighth, ninth, tenth, and even twelfth grade. As you may notice, this was all happening right about the time of the First World War until the Second World War.

The first to apply compulsory state education and to declare homeschooling illegal were the states of the USSR, Germany, and Italy. In the USSR on December 26, 1919, right at the time of the Revolution, Vladimir Lenin introduced a new system of universal compulsory education. Lenin established four years of compulsory elementary education in the countryside and seven years in the cities.

In 1938 on July 6th, the National Socialist leadership under Hitler signed the Law for Schools by which it rendered homeschooling and every other alternative educational method illegal. This law is still on the books. This is still the law, when they go and check, "Is it legal? Is it not legal?" This is the law, from the Nazis, to which they are referring. It essentially has not changed since that time.

In Italy, in 1923, Mussolini and the Minister of Education, Giovanni Gentile, created a new education system suitable for the fascist regime. They made education mandatory up to the age of fourteen. That is what we see eventually happening all over the world, but they were one of the first.

Harsh Repression of Homeschooling by Several European Governments

Right now in Europe—in America this is not the case, thanks be to God—but in Europe it is really a state of war between homeschoolers and a few states, where they have repression. European governments war against parents in order to initiate children into atheism. Germany and Sweden are the most notable.

Germany is the most authoritarian in the world when it comes to education. There is active persecution against homeschooling parents. They have fines, imprisonment, and even abduction of children by the authorities. You can go online and read stories of this. We have one story here of a family who—I think it was in Tennessee—had sought asylum here for a few years, but eventually I think they were forced back to Germany.[11]

In Sweden, there have been some very high-profile cases of the state taking away children who are homeschooled. One in particular I remember where a mother was on her way to the airport, or she was at the airport, and they went and took her child away. To this day, as far as I know, that family has not gotten their child back.[12] There was no other legal claim, except that she was homeschooling. So, this is something that in Europe is still hotly contested, much more than in America.

In the United Kingdom, a law was nearly passed in 2009, the "Children, Schools and Families bill," which would have imposed the most burdensome regulation in the English-speaking world for homeschooling (based on the Badman Review). In 2017, a similar law was introduced for consideration in the Parliament.

In Belgium, the United Nations Convention on Children's Rights has become "the gospel" which homeschoolers must follow.

---

[11] https://www.tennessean.com/story/news/2023/09/29/german-romeike-family-faces-deportation-in-tennessee-what-we-know/70985920007/. As of this publication, the family still battles to stay in the United States by getting extensions on their deportation date as public support and their representative to Congress fights for a more positive outcome.

[12] See here: https://adfmedia.org/press-release/severe-human-rights-violation-sweden-authorities-get-away-child-abduction

United Nations' Convention on the Rights of a Child Document Impinges on Parents' Freedom to Homeschool

Now one of the international documents that has been signed (Convention on the Rights of the Child) that is ostensibly for the sake of the human rights of the child, has within it a lot of language —socialist, communist language—which many people point out is very detrimental and problematic for the freedom of parents to homeschool. So this is something that also exemplifies the struggle, the war against the freedom of parents to raise and teach their children as they see fit. This document has not been enforced in many places, but has been passed by the United Nations. The document:

- Denies parents the right to exempt their children from sexual education class.

- Imposes upon Christian schools the instruction of "other beliefs," and denies them the right to teach that the Church possesses the only true Faith. I think there is something right now in the state of California, a law that would penalize schools and churches, anybody who is paid to teach, if they taught that homosexuality was an abnormality. So it is right now in the State House in California, something similar to what you see here in this document of the United Nations.[13]

- Gives children the ability of choosing their religion, while limiting the power of the parents to only giving advice concerning religion.

---

13 For an update on this, see here: https://www.christianpost.com/news/calif-legislature-approves-measure-criticizing-pastors-for-not-embracing-lgbt-identities.html

- Affirms that children from a young age should be able to decide if they want to go to church or not, even though they are under the guidance and care of their parents.

- Enables the state to intervene in any of the parents' decisions if the authorities judge these decisions were not "in the child's interest." That is exactly what is happening in Sweden. That is the kind of approach the state has for the children that have been taken away.

- Gives children the right of audience with the authorities for every decision of the parents with which the child disagrees.

- Gives children the right to access information on sexual education and abortions, without the knowledge or consent of the parents.

- Denies parents the right of enforcing justified corporal punishment of their children (spanking).

- Denies parents the right of homeschooling. This is the same law that was proposed back in 2009 in the United Kingdom, which actually failed.

General State Education is About the Interest of the State, Not the Children or the Parents

So right now in Europe, there is a crisis in terms of homeschooling, and a lot of repression. J. S. Mills said 250 years ago (by the way, he is no friend of Orthodoxy, nevertheless), "A general State education is a mere contrivance for molding people to be exactly like one another," and "in proportion as it is efficient and successful, it establishes a despotism over the mind, leading by a natural tendency to one over the body."[14] People realized this when this whole movement in the late 1800s for compulsory state education was happening. There were philosophers, there were people in Europe who said "this is not about the interest of the children, this is not about the interest of the parents, this is about the interest of the state, and of forming minds."

IV. Homeschooling is Not an Option; It is a Necessity

Homeschooling is About "Having Faith"; the Survival of Our Christian Identity and the Church

Why am I telling you all this in a talk called "Have Faith"? Well, because it is not just about you and your child. It is actually about the survival of the Church, about the survival of Christian identity, about keeping our children pure from an ever-encroaching demonic system of control. If you see and understand the history of compulsory education, you realize how important it is for us to retain control over the education of the children. It is a matter not just of education, as I said in the beginning, but of faith and of Christian identity and survival.

Three things to consider, as to why homeschooling is so necessary; not an option, but a necessity. State education is run by anti-Christian ideologues who are intent on indoctrination of atheism. It is pretty obvious, I think, in America. In Greece it is perhaps even more obvious in many ways, because we have the stark contrast of a Greek Orthodox culture and society being trampled upon by European and

---

14 John Stuart Mill, *On Liberty*, Ch. 5: Applications. See here https://www.econlib.org/library/Mill/mlLbty.html?chapter_num=5

Have Faith

Greek secular atheist ideology. It is very startling in Greece to see the change within the last twenty years; I was there, and saw the change in 20 years. People who have been there for fifty years have obviously seen this massive change. So, it is very clear to us that the state will be used to impose anti-Christian ideology on the children. That is the first reason why it is essential.

The second reason is that increasingly, public schools no longer educate or form children; rather they deform their souls. I was just talking to a Romanian woman who teaches in a school in Pennsylvania and I asked her, "How is it going in the school there?" and she said, "Well, I am pretty much a babysitter. I go there and I take care of the kids and I make sure they do not hit each other." That is where we have devolved, in terms of state education in many places, because of this dissolution of morality and society. Increasingly, there is no expectation for morality. It is not easy to impart education to children who are not being raised in homes where that is being encouraged.

And number three: instead of being a place of learning, state education is becoming a reform school of the "new man." Just to give you some examples of this: state education today, as we said, is in the hands of anti-Christian forces. It serves to further secularism, which is the spirit of antichrist. It has a monopoly—at least in Europe it does—on education. The rights of parents over the education of their children are violated. The parents become simple spectators, deprived of any sort of control on the education of their children. Obviously we all know also what children go through if they are Christians and they are a minority in a school; we know what they go through in terms of bullying and pressure to conform and go with the broad path. The state actively influences the formation of the conscience, the ethos, and the behavior of the children of Christian parents who reject Christian education at home.

We Homeschool to Remain Faithful to Christ; Public Schools Do Not Equal Education

One of the things that is subtle, but very important, is this ethos, the Orthodox ethos: how is it going to be cultivated when the children do not have examples? This is one of the most important things about educating your child at home, and it is why we have to have faith and be courageous, and remain in this, no matter what outcome we might have educationally. I remember many times with my children, some did better, others did worse. I was on some days a good teacher and on other days a very poor teacher. In some classes I was a terrible teacher and we ended up getting someone else to come in. So there are plenty of reasons to say, "Well, I am not doing the best for my children." But in fact, those are not the first reasons why you homeschool. The education of the child is not the first and foremost reason why we homeschool. So you have to check that—that despair, or that lack of courage, or lack of confidence—and always remember that what we are imparting here is much more. It is not just on the level of the rational. It is not just on the level of the preparation to become a good member of society. It is to remain faithful to Christ.

We said before, also, besides the fact that there is this anti-Christian mentality in the state schools, there is also very poor education, increasingly. And so another reason for avoiding public schools would be the poor education. Schools have ceased being a place for the acquisition of higher knowledge; rather the fleshly man is cultivated. This is seen in many ways. Morals are relativized. The Christian ethos/way is persecuted. Anarchy reigns in minds of children due to immersion in popular culture through the internet and the pervasiveness of immodesty and pornography. The pursuit of Truth is forbidden and this leaves children restless and bored, since they sense the meaninglessness of the utilitarian pursuit of knowledge. Ancient languages (Greek and Latin), which were always at the core of Christian education (since they gave access to the Holy Fathers), are not taught. Hannah Arendt says, "The aim of totalitarian education has never been to instill convictions, but to destroy the capacity to form any conviction."[15]

Then, in this whole creation of the "new man," we see increasingly demonic and blasphemous images and language used; and it is becoming the norm. I was amazed when coming out here on the plane and I was focusing on my talks. I have a man on my left who is a middle-aged man, and man on my right who is a middle-aged man. They both have tablets and they are both watching what I thought would be something a fourteen or fifteen-year-old would probably watch. It was terribly distracting. It was demonic. It was violent. I had to spend four or five hours on this plane, with these two men watching apparently two or three movies of the most demonic and blasphemous images. Now these are grown men; I cannot imagine what the young men and young women who are in the schools today are doing with their tablets, what kinds of things to which kids are being exposed. This is just five hours on a plane. Now over five, ten, fifteen years in the public school, to what are they going to be exposed? So the "new man" that is being formed—the inversion of Christ—and the demonic activity of this "new man," is another basic reason why we need to remain faithful and not lose hope. This totalitarian spirit

---

15 Hannah Arendt, *The Origins of Totalitarianism* (Cleveland, OH: Meridian Books, 1958), p. 468.

and approach of indoctrination also breeds sexual perversity, transgenderism, and all the rest, which is very prevalent today; this exhibits just the total spiritual bankruptcy that we are seeing in the schools today.

Homeschooling Avoids Internet Addiction

Young children are initiated into internet addiction. This is one of the reasons for homeschooling that maybe people do not think about (and one of the things with which I have seen a lot of parents struggle and with which we have also struggled). I do not know how you all are dealing with it, but it is certainly a struggle. Public schooling is initiating children into internet addiction or (to be a bit more specific) "online morphine." When children get exposed at a young age to a computer screen, the addiction that can follow is really destructive for their spiritual life. All around the world—I am sure it is the case here in California— at younger and younger ages, children are getting exposed, and are expected to come to school with their laptop or their tablet, and it becomes a way of life from a very young age. At elementary schools, internet research is being introduced as obligatory. The acquisition and use of a personal computer is increasingly required for many Middle School students. However, it has been shown by a number of studies that this much time on electronic devices is very destructive, not just for their attention span, but for the development of their minds. So another thing that we need to avoid, that we can avoid, and that we should avoid, in home education is the exposure and the addiction of the computer, or the TV screen, or mobile devices, or whatever it is that they might be watching. The main symptoms of "virtual morphine" is unsocial behavior, indifference towards learning, and also aggressive behavior against attempts to decrease their use. So, this is another danger that is present.

Christians Should Plan a Christian Education Future for Their Children Which Forms Their Souls

A Baptist group of the United States with 16 million members are researching a "strategic exodus" from public schools. The Baptists are the largest Protestant confession and the only Christian group in the USA that would not sign the UN's Convention on Children's Rights, on the justification that it deprives parents of their rights, namely, transmitting the faith and teaching at home. This made an impression on me when I was doing research for this: the Baptists have been planning and discussing a mass exodus from public schools for some time. If they understand what is at stake and understand the urgency of homeschooling, then I think the Orthodox should definitely understand it too. It says in this document that I found from the Baptists, "As Christians... we ought to be planning a Christian educational future for our children... Christian parents have a duty to provide their children with a Christian education." Truly in Scripture it is very clear, in the Proverbs and elsewhere, that this is one of the main tasks of the parent—not education per se, but formation of the soul of the child. When we stand before the judgment seat of our Lord, He is not going to ask us if they got into Harvard or if they were lawyers or doctors. He is going to ask us if they were faithful and if they had made progress in purification, illumination and deification. Continuing, the Baptist document says, "A few hours at Sunday school and at church will not have a great influence on the faith and worldview of the child, than the forty or fifty hours a week at public school..." So if the Baptists understand that, then we should too.

Control by the State is Our Future

In my research, it has become apparent that a necessary part of population control by the state is gaining total control of the education of the youth. These are communist, socialist ideas that are behind all state education, even in America. Famously, Fr. Seraphim Rose—he repeated it, I do not know if he actually came up with it—said: "What they experienced in Russia yesterday, we will experience in America today." The reason that is the case is because communism and capitalism are two sides of the same coin. They are both godless, and they are both run by greed and passion and not by virtue. They are also totalitarian in terms of their spirit. One is a political system, and the other is an economic system, but they are both totalitarian. So this spirit of control by the state is very likely to be our future here, or it already is.

The History and Return of the Secret Schools; Preservation of the Faith

Finally, and this is the last thing, before I finish with a few words about faith. We are heading again to the secret schools. Do you know what the secret schools, in Greece, are? They were in the Turkish period. The Christians had secret schools. They were forbidden to have schools by the Turks. So they went underground; they had schools in the churches or in the homes. The priest, or whoever was educated in the community, in the villages, would teach the children using the liturgical books of the Church.

The great educator and apostle to Greece, Saint Kosmas Aitolos, when he preached and went around Greece at the end of this period in the 1700s, said famously to them all, "you must educate your children, open up schools if possible, but educate your children." For the purpose of what? This is what I will get into with my second talk.[16] For the purpose of learning the faith and reading the Scriptures. He did not go around Greece to open up schools so that they might become educated, per se, but so that they might become educated in order to learn the faith. This is where we are headed.

This is why we have to understand that our role is not to have great ideas for our children's educational future, but to be focused on the preservation of the faith, just like St. Kosmas was with the Greeks. That is why we are educating our children. That is the role of education in our life. If it is beneficial and salvific, this is the end goal of their education: to serve their salvation and to serve the Church.

Two Kinds of Faith

Homeschooling is a major part of our struggle to save our children from the hostile environment of contemporary education, which increasingly serves the de-christianization of Orthodox youth, not to mention their stupefaction. It is a place where we create an oasis of Christian formation. Again, as I said, it is not a "personal decision" only. It is an ecclesiastical need. It is not about "better education." It is about salvation. It is about survival as we go forward as Christians. It is a necessary response for anyone who is seeking salvation and seeking to be a true Christian, and to raise true Christians. So, it is imperative for our life, if not for our survival as Orthodox Christians—it is imperative for our spiritual life.

Although we struggle now, day to day (and we are going to struggle, to become better at what we do for our children),

---

16 See the chapter in this book entitled "On the Patristic and 'Post-Patristic' View of Education."

always keep in mind that we are heading into very difficult days, likely of persecution eventually. As each of us continues our struggle here and now, it is equally important that we take some measures for the survival of the Church in the dark days ahead, when the full power of the state will be at the service of Antichrist. If we are going to remain faithful, then we need to come back to our children and go deeper. Homeschooling facilitates all that. We talk about faith a lot—and two words about that— we try to publish a lot of things supporting the Orthodox confession of faith, but many times when we talk about faith, we have in mind this confession of faith. However, there are really two kinds of faith, and both of them are necessary.

The first is a prerequisite for the second. The first kind of faith is the confession of faith that we make as Orthodox Christians, and this is the foundation upon which we can then live a spiritual life. Without this foundation there is no spiritual life. To put it in a figurative way, the confession of the Orthodox faith, which is the presupposition for the spiritual life, can be seen as the fence or the wall around the house of faith, which is trust in God. So, in order for us to go deeper in the life of the Church, we have to first establish these boundaries. That was the term used in the Ecumenical Councils to describe the decisions of the Fathers. It was exactly this word: "*oros*," which is "boundary." So what were the Fathers doing in the Ecumenical Councils? They were laying down the boundaries and they were saying "outside of these boundaries, do not go," because salvation is not attainable. Salvation is the whole reason for the existence of the Church, the whole reason for the Incarnation, the whole reason for everything that Christ did for us. Everything He did for us was for one reason: it was for our salvation. So, everything the Fathers have done, and everything that has been accomplished in the Ecumenical Councils, was for our salvation.

But, that is not enough! The confession of the faith is not enough! We have to go deeper in the spiritual life. We have to go deeper and increase the trust. That is the second kind of faith. So, when we talk about faith, there are two kinds, and both of them are necessary. The second comes about when we go deeper into purification, prayer, and repentance. Then trust increases. You can see this throughout the Scriptures. All of the great miracles of the Lord had as a presupposition faith and repentance.

So, when we approach the Lord, whether it be in the Mysteries, or in our prayer, there are presuppositions. Those are these two kinds of faith: the confession of Him (which is the same thing as saying the Confession of the Orthodox Faith) and then trust in Him (and according to your faith, the miracle happens, as He says in the Gospel). According to our trust in Him, the grace of God is imparted to us in the Holy Mysteries.

So this two-fold faith, have it in mind—in your own life, but also in the life of your children—when you are trying to impart the Orthodox faith in homeschooling. There are always these two aspects that you have to impart to them. They have to understand the boundaries and the foundation of their life, which is the confession of Christ's divine humanity, and His Church. Then they have to go deeper in trusting Him. Then this will be salvation for them.

That is what this image[17] at the end is meant to imply: the passing on of the faith from one generation to another. This is the future of Orthodoxy. It is going to be in the small homes between parents and families, in the small chapels and churches in the catacombs of the future. This is where Orthodoxy is going to flourish. We need to do that. We need to go back to the basics. Thank you very much for your time.

---

17 In the original presentation, the slideshow displayed an image of the painting *The Secret School*. Found on page 15 of this text.

Fr. Peter Heers presenting at the Saint Kosmas Conference
California, April 2018

Q&A SESSION

from "Have Faith: Examining Homeschooling and Compulsory State Education"

QUESTION 1:

It seems like there is a pattern already established by the Church for spiritually and educationally forming our children. Could we, and why do we not, have a pure Orthodox curriculum that could be followed by parents, of course along with the support of a spiritual father?

That is a good question. I am not in the curriculum development business, so I am not sure why there has not—if there has not—been a particular effort made to have a purely Orthodox curriculum. I think that there is not a lot of discussion along the lines of, "What is wrong with classical education as it is?" I do not think many people are saying, "Look, we have got a problem," or, "We have got to refine things." A lot of us are converts. We are bringing in what we know, and there is not a lot of discussion whether any of this is problematic. I am not saying a lot of it is. Our family has used, and we continue to use, Classical Learning Resource

Center. So my talk should not be taken, as I said several times, as just a carte blanche "we do not use it" or "we do not want it" or "we do not read it," but it was trying to give criteria of how and to what degree and in what hierarchy this should go. My talk was an attempt to be a corrective to what I see as going too far in one direction. So I guess what is necessary in terms of a curriculum is a thorough and good discussion on the principles that I laid out—and other principles—of what an Orthodox curriculum should be.

QUESTION 2:

Father Seraphim Rose advocated the use of western music and literature for the cultivation of the soul. We are told of him and of other spiritual fathers having novices read Dickens and Dostoevsky in order to develop normal feelings and warmth of the heart. Would you consider this a proper use of western literature?

First of all, regarding that statement "Father Seraphim Rose advocated the use of western music and literature for the cultivation of the soul"—I will take issue with that. That is not completely accurate. One of the things in the talk that I stressed is that there has to be an application case by case, with discernment. I remember this story from Fr. Seraphim—I was actually thinking about quoting it. The context is that he is dealing with young men coming out of the nihilism of the 60's, and he sees that basic human behavior and normal feelings of kindness and love are not entirely present, and he starts with them where they are. So in that case it is very applicable. But we are talking about Orthodox parents raising children from the get-go in an Orthodox environment to the degree that they enjoy that.

Q&A Session from Have Faith

So the ideal—where do we start? How do we approach this with our own children from a young age? Most of the students going to Fr. Seraphim were late teens at least, if not in their 20's, and so he is starting from where he can with them. I think the context justifies his approach, but I do not know if it would justify that approach in my house or your house, if we have small children who we can raise somewhat differently. Concerning Dickens and Dostoevsky—I do not know if Dostoevsky would be considered western literature. Perhaps; but Dostoevsky is not something I would give to a young person. I think they need to be a mature child of 15 or 16 at least. Dickens, of course, would be applicable. Discernment and the context would determine what literature is appropriate in each case.

I do not know if you can say though, that Fr. Seraphim advocated the use of western music and literature for the cultivation of the soul in the sense of spiritual cultivation. It was more as a preparatory stage, to get to the point of the spiritual life. One of the things I was trying to say in the talk was let us not mistake the spiritual life for the intellectual life, and talk about cultivation of the soul, when we are really talking about cultivation of rational intellect, or the feelings, or things like this. The spiritual life pertains to the spirit of man; it pertains to the *nous*; it pertains to communion with God. That is not the same as the moral life; it is not the same as the intellectual life. One of the problems is to determine what goes where. We have a lot of things, and we are pretty much saying "this is all for the spiritual life," but actually it is not. We have to fit things in rightly, in the right place, and make sense of them.

QUESTION 3:

Please clarify what you include in the category of pagan knowledge and worldly knowledge. Are you speaking about literature only, or other subjects like logic, rhetoric, etc.? Would education of the theologians and orators, and persuasive speaking, logic, etc., be beneficial to our kids in terms of understanding truth and combating fallacy in the world?

We said that the Fathers' approach to literature and philosophy was that it is a tool. It was a practical way to reach people in their day and age, and they used that knowledge as a tool. So absolutely we can use that knowledge as a tool, but not see it as the spiritual life or the end of what we are doing. It is akin to someone who is going to be an orator, they need to learn that practical tool; if someone is going to be a mechanic, or work with wood, obviously he is going to learn to work with those tools. It is on that level that we are seeing things like oration and the honing of the mind for logic. That is definitely applicable and acceptable, but again, in its place and for its purpose.

QUESTION 4:

Could you talk a little bit about why St. Basil, being raised in a pious Christian family, went off unbaptized to study pagan wisdom?

In the fourth century, there was a waning practice among Christians not to be baptized as infants. I am not sure exactly why St. Basil was not. He was from a very pious family; his grandmother, his mother, his sister, were all pious people, and they had martyrs in their family. So, I am not sure why his family practiced this. It was somewhat common, but it did wane, and the Church did frown on it, and it eventually ended. We do not hear much about it in other saints as time goes on. It was partly out of reverence and fear of God, because they took baptism so seriously. They said when you were baptized, you have to live a different life. Somewhat like when someone becomes a monk, or in the monasteries when someone becomes a great schema monk. They take it so seriously that they have to change their life, and change their ways. That is part of why people approached baptism with such fear of God, and they put it off. But I do not have a better answer than that, of why St. Basil's family followed that path.

QUESTION 5:

What is the value, if any, of studying ancient, or modern philosophy at the upper school or college level?

As I have said before, the value is, if someone has been well-grounded in the life of the Church, the Lives of the Saints, if they have approached the Scriptures and the saints and been grounded in that, if they have understood the Orthodox *ethos* to some degree as children, and have acquired an Orthodox *phronema* as much as possible, then there is a maturity to look at other forms of literature and philosophy. If that is judged as appropriate for that particular child, and beneficial, then that would be applicable to college or high school. But it has to be on a case by case basis. The understanding should not be that every child does this because that is how you are cultivated and become a spiritual person, or a refined Christian. That is problematic, because that implies that this particular form of education—the honing of the mind, and logic, and understanding philosophical terms—is somehow a universal need of every Christian, and part of the spiritual development of every Christian, which is not the case. Maybe I have given the impression that I am rejecting these, and I am not. I am just rejecting an extreme view of them, and an imbalance.

QUESTION 6:

How would you define the Greek word "παιδεία" (paideia)? What components of development does it encompass? Does it encompass spiritual formation? Is there any better word in Greek to describe the education and formation of a child?

How would you define the Greek word "παιδεία" (paideia)?

It is defined as the rearing of a child, the training or instruction of a child, education. There are actually several words that define it; the result is a learning culture, a mental culture. St. Paul uses the word in Scripture in many places—in Ephesians, Timothy, Hebrews—and it is used usually as chastening or discipline in those contexts. So that is the word "*paideia.*"

What components of development does it encompass?

It is a general term for whatever goes into raising children and instructing them.

Does "paideia" encompass spiritual formation?

Yes, but not usually. When we speak about spiritual formation we do not really use the word "paideia," maybe spiritual formation (μόρφωση) or spiritual life (πνευματικότητα). I do not think there is an equivalent of *"paideia"* just for spiritual pursuits; it does not come to mind, in any case.

Is there any word in Greek to better describe the total education and formation for a child than "paideia"?

No, I do not think so. Although, it is not usually thought of as pertaining to spiritual formation.

QUESTION 7:

What should be the classical language of choice? Why are most Orthodox classical educators in America pushing Latin over Greek? What are the advantages of having Orthodox children learn Greek over Latin?

The obvious advantage is that the Holy Scriptures are written in Greek. The Old Testament Septuagint is in Greek, the Church Fathers are in Greek—I mean there are a lot of reasons why we should be studying Greek and not Latin. I am not sure why most classical educators prefer Latin. Maybe this is indicative of the problem we have in America, that we are approaching classical education in a passive way, and so when we see everybody else doing Latin, we think, "Well, let us do it too." Not that I am against Latin—my son is in his sixth year of Latin, but he is also in his sixth year of Greek. If I were to choose between the two, I would choose Greek, because it is going to open up more to him, in terms of access to the Fathers and the Scriptures. So I think absolutely, in an Orthodox context, Greek is preferable.

And you know, interestingly, there are not a lot of texts in Latin in terms of Orthodoxy, very few. Even though

Latin was taught in Constantinople until the seventh or eighth century, nobody was writing in Latin. Some people think that Latin was only taught in the West, but no; in Constantinople and in the schools in the east, they taught Latin as well as Greek, and it was actually even used for a time in certain aspects of the Empire in the east. So, even though some of the Fathers were learning Latin and people were being taught Latin in the east, they were not using it to theologize.

QUESTION 8:

I have heard the words "heart," "nous," "eye of the soul," and today "spirit" used in close association. Are these terms synonymous? If distinct, how are they different? Is the term "phronema" distinct from the terms above? How does the phrase "mind of Christ" relate to these other terms?

Regarding "heart," "nous," "eye of the soul," and "spirit" used in close association:

That is right, those are almost synonymous. The heart and the *nous* are not synonymous, but "*nous*," "eye of the soul," and "spirit" are pretty much describing the same thing. There are shades of difference.

If distinct, how are they different?

It has to do with usage, where they are used. In Scripture, you find the word "spirit" used, and it means what the Fathers mean by "*nous*." St. Paul talks about the "spirit" crying out,[18] so in that context that is essentially what the Fathers mean by the term "*nous*." For "eye of the soul," this

18 Galatians 4:6

also is a term referring to the *nous*; it is not talking about the rational intellect, or the imagination, or the feelings, but it is talking about the *nous*—you might call it "spiritual intellect." Intellect could have been a perfectly good word, if it had not been ruined by heterodox theology, and we could have had that intellect/mind—with mind being the rational function of the soul, and intellect being the equivalent of the *nous*. But because there is such confusion in English, most Orthodox translations have chosen "*nous*." You could also refer to it as the "spirit of man."

Is the term "phronema" distinct from the terms above?

Yes. "*Phronema*" is essentially the worldview or outlook, the mindset. So we are definitely talking here about the rational intellect, the way we think, the way we understand things, the way we look at the world. The Orthodox *phronema* is usually referring to the way we understand things theologically; it goes along with theology essentially.

How does the biblical phrase "mind of Christ" relate to these other terms?

We talked about that this afternoon, in the passage from St. Paul. He ends this great quote that we took from Corinthians, by saying we have the mind of Christ.[19] However, the context is talking about the Spirit of God, and he says in particular, "that which is of God is revealed to us by His Spirit; even so, no man knoweth the things of God but the Spirit Who is of God. We speak not in the words which man's wisdom teacheth, but those which the Holy Spirit teacheth, comparing spiritual things with spiritual. But the natural man receiveth not the things of the Spirit

---

19   I Corinthians 2:16

of God, for they are foolishness to him, neither can he know them, because they are spiritually discerned."[20] So here, "the mind of Christ," in this context, the way I understand it, is referring to the *nous*, the acquisition of the mind of Christ. It is not referring to the created order, but the uncreated, through communion with God and the revelation of the Holy Spirit. So acquiring the mind of Christ does not mean that you become really adept at philosophy or theology, but that you enter into the mystery, and it is revealed to you—you could perhaps say, intuitively (though I think this word is loaded in English today), so maybe say, experientially acquired. That is a good point, to make this distinction between "*phronema*" and "the mind of Christ," which would be interesting to develop.

You said that "heart" and "nous" are not synonymous, so can you explain this more?

The heart is the center of man. We talk about the *nous* descending into the heart, and the heart being the center of man, both the physical and the spiritual. So in that sense they cannot be synonymous.

So, in this context [of the nous descending into the heart], the heart is not simply metaphorical? It actually means the heart?

Yes. The Fathers talk about the actual physical heart being also the center of man, spiritually.

QUESTION 9:

My son is thinking about going into psychology. What are your thoughts on how to choose a school

---

20   Cf. I Corinthians 2:10–14

for that field of study, and what are your recommendations for how to navigate through the messed-up thought in that field?

In my presentation today, I talked about issues pertaining to the study of ancient philosophy and contemporary literature. These issues are even more exacerbated with psychology—even more problematic—because psychology is a field that from the get-go was not at all consistent with the Christian understanding of man. Somebody who is going into psychology is going to have to do a lot of revision of what they are learning, and that means they are going to need a very Orthodox understanding. If they do not have that, they are bound to be confused. So there needs to be a lot of effort on his part, when he encounters things, to take refuge in Orthodox sources to make sense of it, otherwise he could come out after four years being very confused, and led astray (since there are thousands of theories that are presented in contemporary psychology which are not consistent with the anthropology of the Orthodox Church). Psychology does not recognize the things we are talking about here: the *nous* or even the soul.

I am not sure what is drawing him there. I would ask him what he is thinking about, what is it he wants to do, if he wants to serve his fellow man, and help him? If he was here, I would ask him to talk about it a little bit and examine why he wants to do it. I am sure he has thought about it. I would just be interested to learn. Maybe he is thinking it is akin to theology or philosophy and it is interesting to explore, or he wants to learn about himself?

He is interested in people and their behavior, why they do what they do, he finds it fascinating, he is interested in personality testing and finds it helpful to understand himself.

If he was here I would want to talk with him and say, "You need to sit down and do some serious study of Orthodox anthropology before you start learning all this."

In high school he did a Socratic discussion type program through a Protestant university, Biola, and he got into C.S. Lewis there. So he knows C.S. Lewis well.

C.S. Lewis is an interesting figure in contemporary Orthodox America. I have been gone for eighteen years, so I am new to Orthodoxy in America, in a way. After my conversion to Orthodoxy, I was here in America for 6 years, and then 18 years in Greece. Now back in America, I notice how much people are interested in his writings. As a former Anglican, I grew up with C.S. Lewis; my mother read us The Chronicles of Narnia. However, coming back as an Orthodox Christian from Greece and having studied dogmatic theology, it is clear that his theology presents many problems. He has a lot of errors, which people do not talk about, which is also curious.

Could you write some books about that?

(Laughs) Well, I mean, he has got a lot of great things, but he has got a lot of problems too. First of all, his ecclesiology is heretical. He does not believe in the one Church. The fact that *Mere Christianity* is a great seller should make you pause. It is very much of the 20th century, his understanding of the Church. But his anthropology is off too. He is following western anthropology; he is following Aquinas. He is not even well-versed in that. He is not a theologian. So I would say whenever we are dealing with anyone outside of the patristic tradition of the Orthodox Church, you have got to go with a critical spirit and say, "What is going on here? Let us be bees." Right? At least be bees! Nevertheless, I would say there is so much Orthodox material today compared with what there was twenty years ago when I left for Greece, that one does not need to run as much to non-Orthodox sources. If for some reason we are [going to non-Orthodox sources], we need to go with a critical spirit [analyzing it from the perspective of the Orthodox *phronema*], but that presupposes we know Orthodox theology and Orthodox anthropology, and most of us do not. So, it creates problems.

In our culture today, a lot of people are hungering for Orthodox psychologists and some priests want the assistance of Orthodox psychologists...

To me, that is the sign of a fall in Orthodox spirituality. Psychologists are a far cry from spiritual fathers, but that is how people are thinking about them. They are not going to provide the healing for which people are searching. They are going to provide a little help. They are not useless, but they are not anywhere near what the Church can offer and should be offering in terms of spiritual help.

QUESTION 10:

I have just begun the book Orthodox Psychotherapy. Is that a different vein from what we are discussing here regarding Orthodox psychologists?

Regarding *Orthodox Psychotherapy*, the term is not referring to psychology at all. It is presenting patristic teaching by Metropolitan Hierotheos Vlachos. He uses that term in its real meaning—"psycho" and "therapy" the healing of the soul—not the mind. So think about what we talked about, how the mind is not the organ with which we commune with God. Honing your mind and making it a powerful tool is not the spiritual life, or even the beginning of the spiritual life. Think about all we said, and then think about psychology. They are dealing on the level of the mind, and then they are talking about healing the soul. They are not even beginning to heal the soul, because they do not even understand what the soul is.

I do not want to oversimplify things, but generally the approach is very lacking. So the fact that we as Orthodox Christians are very interested in going to Orthodox psychologists to me says there is a serious problem in the Orthodox Church among Orthodox Christians: we are looking for health from a science which is not based on the Orthodox tradition. Now are there Orthodox psychologists who are doing it in an Orthodox manner? Maybe, perhaps. Maybe there are some examples. I am not familiar with them, but maybe there are. I am sure there are. Generally speaking, however, that would be the problem with this approach.

The examples of holy elders in the twentieth century are many, we can go to them, we can read them. We can see what it means to be a healer of the soul. We have Saints Porphyrios, and Paisios, and Iakovos. We have many examples. We do not need to do guesswork. Let us pick up those books, and let us study them closely, to find out from them what it means to be a healthy human being. We can do that—it is all in English now, we do not have to go searching for non-Orthodox sources.

QUESTION 11:

How does one remove harmful literature from the home without causing the children to turn away from God in rebellion? How do I avoid the introduction of what I think is not useful to my younger children by older siblings?

Well... there might have to be rebellion. I am not sure you can avoid it. If there is a blatant violation of the family environment, and if they are affecting other children with this literature or whatever it might be, then it is not a personal issue. In such a case, I think that the rule or the law has to be laid down for the sake of the child. I will tell you what I tell my children: "As long as you are here, until you are gone from this house, this is the way things are going to be in this house. When you are gone, if you want to change that, that is up to you; but as long as you are here, until you are eighteen or twenty—whenever you decide to go on, and get married, or whatever you are going to do—this is the way it works here." If that means they are going to be rebelling, let them rebel.

I know there are extreme cases where maybe kids become violent, or reactionary, and so there needs to be lots of prayer and lots of patience. But it is very detrimental for children to acquire that kind of boldness, ultimately, because it will affect their fear of God and the humility that they need to have before God, if they have cultivated that already with their mother and father. But I do not know if there is any magic bullet that is going to make things easy if a child is disposed to rebel, and is not listening to the mother and father. It is going to be a process of much prayer, patience, but also giving order to the house. Ultimately, most of the time, they want that. They are actually seeking that, in a roundabout way, yearning for it. Maybe what is missing in a lot of these cases is prayer, falling on your knees, and begging God to soften the child's heart. I think most of us could increase that; I know I can.

Question 12:

Does Christian fantasy, like Tolkien and C.S. Lewis, fall into the same category as mythology, in terms of what you described in your talk earlier today?

Yes, I think it does fall into the same category, for two reasons. One is that it is fantasy literature, and the closest that I can get to its equivalent in the ancient world is mythology. It is pretty close to mythology; and mythology is probably on the list of ancient texts that they would have exposed young men to—not small children, not eight-year-olds, but young men. That list would have been philosophy, poetry, and then maybe mythology. So, for that reason I do think that it falls into that category. The redeeming factor, at least more so in Lewis which is allegory, is that these are attempts to communicate messages of virtue and valor. So there is that redemptive aspect in them. There was also that in ancient mythology, although less so.

The problem here is—and I did not get into this in my talk because it would have been another entire talk—in the Orthodox tradition there is definitely a very negative stance among all Church Fathers towards the imagination and the cultivation of the imagination. It is throughout the ascetic literature. Now there is some debate as to why they were against it, and if the reasons they were against it is applicable to contemporary fiction.

Metropolitan Hierotheos Vlachos has an article on the imagination, and in it he specifically says—and we are talking about the cultivation of the spiritual life—that the cultivation of the imagination is essentially opposed to cultivating, in the *nous*, communion with God. So, someone might say, "Well, that is different than what is happening in fiction," and I am not prepared to give a response to that.

I am inclined to say that it is problematic; that such a distinction does not really hold water. It is still the imaginative faculty that is being cultivated. Now how you use your imagination, obviously, is important, right? However, cultivating the imagination is a problem if you are interested in the spiritual life. Now, if you are not interested in the spiritual life, then cultivate away (in that case, it is not a problem); but we are here as Orthodox Christians and we are saying that the end goal is to commune with God. Anything that is going to take us away from that, we should be at least reticent about; we should at least be on guard.

    I do think there is room for pastoral condescension, and dealing with people where they are. Fr. Seraphim Rose used Dostoevsky, or actually Dickens more, with those young men. For someone interested in becoming a monk, however, that is probably not the kind of literature on which you would want to spend too much time. You would want to get past that. Maybe that was necessary for them, and I think you could say something analogous with children. If you see that pastorally there is some kind of need, then maybe there is some room for that. It is generally problematic—in the context of the spiritual life—to cultivate the imagination. Whether there is room pastorally to condescend, as St. Basil did with the youths in the fourth century, or as Fr. Seraphim Rose did in the twentieth century, that really depends on a case by case basis. There cannot be a general rule across the board: "Do not do this."

    Some do say they are edified by Lewis and Tolkien. I tend to think that the amount of edification that they are going to get is rather minimal compared to what they could get if they were investing themselves in the literature of the Church. That is my two cents on that. I intentionally did not address that during the talk because I could have written another entire talk just on that topic alone. I was preparing to talk about it, but I decided it was impossible to address it all in one talk.

Question 13:

What do you feel would be an appropriate age to begin reading the Scriptures to children? My oldest is nine but sometimes when I try to read to them, it does not go how I hope.

What are you reading from? [The Gospels.] Do you have a book that is for children, with pictures? You have got to keep their attention, obviously, and you need to start with stories, and get them interested. You can start at a very young age. In our home, we read the Scriptures to a three-year-old or a four-year-old and they sit and listen. It is not an Orthodox Bible, but it has pictures of the scenery. You do not have to worry about the translation for four, five, or six-year-olds. King James would be the most traditional English translation; I do not think it is surpassed except by some of the Orthodox attempts. Language matters. The degree of refinement in language matters if you are going to communicate things from the Scriptures.

Question 14:

Do you find it helpful to have a dedicated place for your children to do homeschooling, or is the kitchen table fine?

Well, it depends on your house. In our house in Greece, we had a whole area dedicated to homeschooling, and then we had an area where we usually sit and read, and we try to make that a place for the kids that is inviting and comfortable. We practice what the monks do in the monastery: we read during the meal. We read the Lives of the Saints, or we read the lives of contemporary elders from Mt. Athos, and that is something that the kids like—or most of the kids. One of my children does not like it, but he is so reactionary that he will start off saying, "No, I don't want to read that," and at the end, he will say "OK, let's read another one." Sometimes you just have to push through and not listen to your children very much. Whatever it is, start it out, and be persistent. There is a tendency to allow the children to lead us. We think, "Oh, they do not want to hear it, OK, I will stop." No! Do not stop, keep reading. Maybe show them an example for a month or two, of you reading with your wife, or with whoever is going to listen. Then eventually say, "This is the program, this is what we are going to do." Make it exciting, as much as you can. Say, "This is going to be really interesting." Choose some stories in the beginning that are really interesting, that will keep their attention. Then it is a matter of just plowing through, being consistent, making sure that this becomes a tradition—something we do every day, every week—and not paying attention to the inconsistency of the children. Children are inconsistent; you cannot be affected too much by their inconsistency.

QUESTION 15:

At what age should we start reading to them the Lives of the Saints?

As soon as they can start following it and sit still. It depends on the child. If a three or four-year-old can sit still, you can read a little bit to them. Whatever you can get in. Whatever you can do. Another thing you can do is just take excerpts, little tiny stories, for the younger children. I do not think there is any reason why you cannot start early. Find

Potamitis' books. We have those in Greece, but I think they are available in America too. Potamitis has all these little Lives of the Saints. That is where you should probably start with the very young children.

Does everyone have a complete collection of the Lives of the Saints? There are three or four versions now in English. If you do not, that is something that you should make a point to buy. There is a five-volume set from Ormylia in Greece; there is the set by St. Dimitri of Rostov; there is the Great Synaxarion; so there are at least three different sets of the Lives of the Saints available in English. If you do not have those and that is not a part of your reading list for yourself and your children, you should definitely get them. It is basic food for everyone, but especially for the young children. I think that is what they should be reading first and foremost—the Scriptures and the Lives of the Saints—throughout their life, but especially as part of their curriculum in the early years. It is something that should definitely be part of their daily spiritual and intellectual food—and not just here and there, but every day.

QUESTION 16:

My personal reading of the Lives of the Saints has come only from the big books that you buy of an individual saint. Are you talking about something that is concise for each saint?

Yes. The set I have in mind that our family uses is from Ormylia, the monastery in Greece, and it is called the Synaxarion. Every day of the year we have certain saints we commemorate on that day. There are longer versions of all these lives, but in this collection from Ormylia they will give a fairly long version for the major saints—anywhere from three to five or even seven to eight pages, but nothing like 50 or 100 pages. So every day you are going to get a short life of the saints of the day—some just a few lines, others a few pages. So you are living with them and you are reading them as you go throughout the liturgical year. I think it is the best way to approach them, and then when you want to go deeper, you can search out a fuller life for the saint.

Question 17:

There was a time in my life when I tried to completely cut off all non-Orthodox things and it drove me a little bit crazy because I was constantly questioning, "Is that Orthodox? Is it not Orthodox? Who is the author?" I feel like I was being a little too paranoid. So, I am trying to understand: Is it prescriptive or is it not a set rule?

No, there is not a rule. I would say that you should try to focus more on what you should fill yourself up with as opposed to focusing on what you are trying to avoid. Think of it positively, and go deeper. And do not worry so much about trying to shut out everything that does not have an "O" over the entryway. That is not to say that we should be indiscriminate—or without discrimination—but there does not need to be a paranoia if something does not have an Orthodox label. There are actually things that are labeled "Orthodox" which are not very Orthodox, so the label is not a very good criterion.

You have got to obtain discernment, and that is only going to be done by going deeper. The best thing is to read the Lives of the Saints, Scripture, and books on prayer. Until we begin to pray and to make progress in prayer—especially the Jesus prayer—we are going to be limited to how much of the grace of God we are going to be able to receive. It is like a small cup; it can only hold so much. We are going to be thirsty, but we are not going to be able to drink from the well, because we need to enlarge our heart, and that happens through prayer. That happens through opening ourselves up and communicating with God. As long as we are always communicating with ourselves, our thoughts, other people, and the created world, we are going to remain a limited vessel. So, you have to go deeper, and that means mainly prayer.

We need to learn from the saints and be inspired by them in terms of how to pray and how to commune with God and how to struggle. Because when you read the Lives of the Saints, one of the first things—and best thing—that results is that you become inspired to struggle, inspired to deny the passions, and inspired to imitate them. That is why we read the Scriptures; that is why we read the Lives of the Saints. We do not read the life of the saint just to celebrate the life of the saint; it is not just a feast day to go and eat and remember a saint. The whole point of the festal calendar—the lives of the saints that we read and the services that were written—is for one reason: to imitate the saints and to follow them. So every time we celebrate a saint, we should be thinking, "How can I imitate this person? What can I learn?"

Most of us spend our lives going broader on a horizontal plane and not going deeper. We acquire knowledge about the Church, about God, about the spiritual life, but we do not actually begin to live the spiritual life because we do not learn to pray. We do not learn to struggle. This is especially problematic in America because a lot of us are intellectuals, and we have come to the Church through intellectual reading and study. We think that if we can continue to become experts in everything Orthodox, that means we are doing well spiritually, but it does not mean that. That does not matter. There are people who are very well versed in Orthodoxy, and they teach in universities, and they have a miserable spiritual life—miserable! They have problems in their family. I have seen it in Thessaloniki. It does not matter what you know. You can become an expert and become well-versed; but it does not mean you have begun the spiritual life. I could stand here and tell you wonderful things and go home and be a wreck spiritually. There is no proof of my spiritual life, just because I can stand up here and talk about it. Just because I have developed my rational intellect and become good at it—that is not the spiritual life. We are not even beginning the spiritual life with that; we are preparing. I could be very well prepared; I have learned everything I need to know. Think about Church history; think about the Scriptures; people were close to Christ—they saw Christ; they heard Christ—yet they denied Him. They were not lacking access to Christ—so what is missing? It is obviously something else. It is something deeper. Just acquiring knowledge is not enough. It is important; it is a preparatory stage, but it is not the spiritual life.

We need to go deeper, we need to go vertical. That is not an issue of education as much as it is going inward and acquiring self-knowledge. We said earlier the key to acquiring self-knowledge is having a spiritual father. The spiritual father's role is to show us ourselves, reveal to us the will of God, and be that mirror. You can see that in the spiritual life—with the spiritual father as a guide—the knowledge of God and the knowledge of self are interconnected. The more you know of God, the more you understand yourself; the more you understand yourself, the easier it is to draw close to God. In Greek we call it "*θεογνωσία*" (*theognosia*) which is God-knowledge and "*αυτογνωσία*" (*aftognosia*) which is self-knowledge. These two things go hand in hand, like two wings. If you are living alone or are living with people who have no sense of the spiritual life, and there is no self-knowledge being cultivated, you could live your whole life and never see your passions, and think you are perfectly fine, because you have not begun the process of acquiring self-knowledge.

This is really the process of repentance, is it not? When do we repent? When we come to ourselves. The prodigal "came to himself" it says in the Scriptures. What does that mean? It means he came to self-knowledge. He understood where he was in relation to God. So he said, "Why am I here? I will get up and I will go back." Therefore, self-knowledge was a prerequisite for him to return to God. What is return? Repentance. If people do not have self-knowledge, they will never repent. They will never return to God, right?

That is the great tragedy with most people, even people in the Church. I had people in my church—coming to church on Sunday—who had almost zero self-knowledge. They would say to me, "I am really a good person, Father. I do not need to go to confession." Of course, that means he is totally blind—entirely blind to himself and has no self-knowledge—and he feels no need to return to God. He does not even understand what he is missing. That is a tragic place to be.

So, we have got to go deeper, acquire self-knowledge, and submit ourselves to a spiritual father who will then reveal ourselves to us, and then we can begin on the path of repentance. This is the spiritual life. Most of what passes as spiritual life is not the spiritual life. It is learning *about* the spiritual life.

QUESTION 18:

At what age do you recommend that children start confessing?

It varies according to the child, but anywhere from five to eight-years-old. You can start early. At five-years-old it is not going to be much of a confession, but just getting them going and talking to the elder or spiritual father. Explain to the child, "This is part of our life, this is our spiritual father, he loves us, we love him," and do whatever you need to do pedagogically to prepare the child that this is a very basic thing in our life.

That relationship is going to be very helpful to you when they grow up and they are teenagers. It is going to save you from many headaches because you are going to say, "I do not know; go speak to your spiritual father." There are going to be times when you think, "If I say 'no' to this child, he is going to go ballistic, or he is going to say this, or who knows what." So, instead you can say, "You have to be obedient to your spiritual father; you need to go talk to him." [audience laughs] It is funny on the one hand, but it is really true, and very, very helpful.

One of the things that was a huge problem for me in leaving Greece was exactly that: I had to leave my spiritual father. It has been very difficult. You cannot really have a spiritual father far away. I know Fr. Demetrios said you can have a spiritual father far away—you can, but you cannot. You need to see the person. It is a different relationship when you are sitting face to face. My spiritual father is on Mt. Athos, and he said, "If you are leaving Greece, you have to find another spiritual father in America." The personal relationship is really basic. You have got to go.

Now in America, things are very much harder geographically. There are fewer of them, and it is harder to get to them, so we have to make more of an effort. However, you can maintain a healthy spiritual life just seeing your spiritual father twice or three times a year—it is possible. You write a lot of letters.

One of the things I recommend to everybody—if they are not doing it—especially the children, is to keep a little booklet. They should keep a little notepad with them, and when they fall into sins or when they have questions, they write them down. If you do not do that—over the two or three or four month period that you are going to be gone from your spiritual father—you will go with a blank notepad. Because it is just impossible for all of us to remember everything that we want to talk to him about. We do not have to go with everything, but it is a picture. Just that practice helps us acquire self-knowledge, because you begin to see a pattern. You write down each sin: I just got angry, oops—I got angry again, oh—I got angry again. And you come to realize, "I have a passion of anger. It is not just once in a while. Look how many times I did it? Forty-four times in the three months I fell into sin and I got really angry at my wife." So, then you can see you have got a passion of anger, and you go to the elder and you say, "I did that forty-four times!" And he will say, "OK, here is what we have got to do", and he can work with you. If you go there and say, "Oh, I get angry once in a while", and you do not really understand the seriousness of your passion, that is not going to be profitable. So, cultivating confession from a young age is important, but also doing it right. It is not just, "Let us go to the spiritual father, ha, ha, ha," and then we go home again. That is not self-knowledge. Half of the benefit that we get from going to the spiritual father is the work we did before we went to him.

We need to realize that all the Mysteries—including confession, communion, ordination, everything in the Church, even the smaller things like the service of the small blessing of the water, or whatever it might be—have presuppositions. Depending on our stance and depending on our preparation, the grace of God visits us. So, if we do not have preparation, if we have no fear of God, if we have no prayer, then we go and we leave as we went. It depends on us. God is there. He is there in every Mystery, but He is not there for us if we are not prepared, and if we are not going with a broken heart, and repentance, and prayer. That is very clear in the Gospels. Everyone who walked away with a miracle came with a broken heart, with a prayerful heart, with a repentant heart, with a faithful heart. These presuppositions are oftentimes not talked about very much, and are not cultivated, and therefore the grace of God is not visiting us as it should and could.

This always made an impression on me on Mt. Athos. I went many times to Mt. Athos and I was present at a few baptisms. People come from all over the world to Mt. Athos and many times they return to their country after spending months there and after being baptized. In some cases, the grace of God was very present in the face of the person who was baptized, in the whole community, and in the whole monastery. The way I came to understand this is that this person had become worthy of this manifestation. It does not mean that God was not present in every baptism, but it was manifested in this baptism because that person came in prepared ascetically. What is another word for that? Purification. Purification does not begin after baptism—well, it does in a way, that is when you are made new—but it also begins even in the preparation of the baptism. Even as a catechumen, the process of purification begins. It is not to the same degree or the same quality before baptism as afterwards, but it exists.

All of the Mysteries have these presuppositions and depending on our stance, we will enjoy the grace of God. I think that is a missing ingredient here in America, and not many people stress that. A lot of people go to communion every week; they are in the Church thirty years, and they are not changing. There is something wrong. The Church is a place of healing. If you have not come to greater self-knowledge and greater communion with God after twenty years of being in the Church, and you are communing regularly, then you are probably doing something wrong.

Question 19:

We are very strict about what we let our kids watch. We do not let them watch very many of the Disney movies. They have seen very few movies that are rated above PG. Some G movies we do not let them see because some of those cartoons are just terrible. How do I encourage them so that they do not feel bitter or resentful? How do I help them avoid feeling like they are missing out on something?

How old are your children?

[They range from 3 to 14 years old.]

Is the 14-year-old also in this category?

[She has been allowed to see a few other movies, when we have watched them with her, so that we could discuss the parts. The issue is now they are going to Orthodox camps, and are being influenced by other Orthodox kids. They are coming home and

> saying things like, "Why can I not do this or that?" For example, they are saying things like, "Why can I not watch *The Little Mermaid*? It is just a cartoon. They are making fun of us because we have not seen *The Little Mermaid*." I say, "Just go ahead and say, 'Well, you know, my mom is just that way,' and let it go."]

That is a good answer. What is the question? Are you doubting your pedagogy?

> [No. My question is: how do I encourage them so that they do not feel bitter or resentful? How do I help them avoid feeling like they are missing out on something?]

You could expose them to something that the other children are not exposed to—I do not know what that might be—maybe some really good literature or something. It is always movies today, is it not? Everything has to be visual, but as much as you can, avoid the visual, for as long as you can. Expose your kids to something else, and then send them back to their friends to say, "I did not see *Little Mermaid*, but you have not read this book that I read with my mom, and you are missing out too."

Instead of always having this inferiority complex—and thinking, "I have got to do what everybody else does"—we need to be fools for Christ today. Fools for Christ intentionally provoke other people to judge them. That is what fools for Christ do. Does everybody know what a fool for Christ is? Are you familiar with this? It is often referred to as the highest form of sanctity in the Orthodox Church. It is people who have reached such degrees of sanctity that they live as if fools to the world and their actions appear mysterious and do not make sense, but actually many times they do make sense because they are clairvoyant as well. We need to live like fools for Christ today. In other words, we need to learn how—in the face of this *zeitgeist*—to teach our children to resist this spirit of pressure to conform and to go with the masses. This happens even on the level of the young children, and that is really where it all begins. This is why people, when they reach age twenty, have lost all sense of direction, because they have given in to this again and again, and their value is in what other people are going to tell them to do, essentially. They have lost direction. You have got to fight against that. You can fight against it by essentially ridiculing it.

I used to ridicule the secular society, ridicule the mentality, and expose it for what it was, so that my children would not feel an inferiority complex before the world. You could say for instance, "Why would I want to watch some stupid movie about something that does not even exist? Some half-man, half-fish? What is this?!" Instead of saying, "Oh, I am sorry," and being so apologetic. Why do we have to be apologetic? We always have this approach, as if we have to apologize for not being like everybody else.

Teach them to look at what they are doing. Tell the child, "If it is good, let us do it. Tell me what is good about it, and I will send you tomorrow to do it." Get them to analyze it, instead of just accepting it at face value and saying, "That is a good thing since everybody is doing it." That is the implication: it is good because all the children are doing it. Ask, "What is it? What are they doing?" "Oh, everybody has their nose pierced." "And? That is what they used to do in Africa when they did not have Christianity and they were not educated. This is something that comes from tribal practice." Say whatever you want to say, but do not allow it to become a given that we need to feel that we are missing out.

Convey to them, "It is the others that are missing out. The others are doing things that are not according to the Image and the Likeness. You are special because you are a Christian," and rejoice in it instead of being ashamed. I am not saying we are ashamed of being Christians, but that is what the world wants. The spirit of the world wants us to reply apologetically, and we should not. We do not have to apologize for being Christian.

The other problem with this is that if you have an older child who has lost his way a bit, or has rebelled, or is in a rebellious state, and you give in to these pressures, because they are being pressured, you will pay for it with the younger children. Stand your ground, because it will become much harder. The younger ones are watching you. "What is mom doing with him? What is he doing? How is mom going to respond to that?" The consequences are exponential as time goes on.

My son came back a couple of days ago and said, "Everybody in the world—every single human being, about fourteen zillion, billion people"—I cannot remember what number he used, but it was something like that—"Fourteen zillion people are playing this particular video game." I said to him, "Really? The numbers matter? There are millions of people who have rejected Christ!", and I started to reason with him and say, "That is not criteria." The kids need to learn how to think.

We have to react proactively and not be ashamed, and not be at all afraid to be different. The irony of it is there are so many kids out there who are doing exactly that to get attention. They are doing the thing that nobody else is doing, to get attention, and yet, we are afraid to be Christians and to be something different. Why? It is very serious, actually, because on one level you can say, "Oh, it is just a mermaid"—but it is not. It is a pattern of wanting to conform to the culture, and if that starts, it becomes a way of life at fifteen or twenty. It is very important to nip it in the bud.

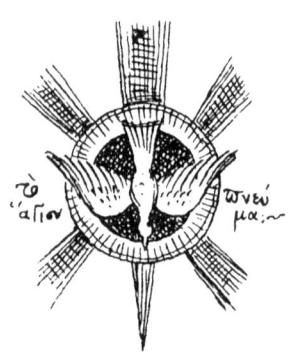

The very small church of *Panagia Megalomata*
(location of a "secret school")

St. Paisios of the Holy Mountain

CHAPTER II

Seeking Truth: Forming Children in the Love of Truth

Lecture delivered at the
St. Kosmas Orthodox Homeschool Conference
"Educating Children Within an Orthodox Ethos"
November 8-11, 2018
St. Nicholas Ranch, Dunlap, CA

Venerable Fathers, Esteemed Colleagues, Brothers and Sisters, Christ is in our Midst!

Our discussion today is concerned with how we as parents and as teachers can form our children in the love of Truth. In unpacking this for you, it is apparent we must:

1. Determine of <u>what</u> the love of truth consists and why it is necessary for us to impart it.

2. Determine <u>the way</u> in which we impart truth to our children.

Of What the Love of Truth Consists and Why It Is Necessary For Us To Impart It

To determine of what the love of Truth consists we have nowhere else to turn but to the Incarnate Truth, Who is Love and Who first loved us. We find Him in the divine record of His Coming, the Holy Scriptures, and in the continuation of His Incarnation in the Church, in the lives of the "little Christs,"[21] who were made Him by His Grace.

Our love for Christ can be expressed in an endless amount of ways. In the Lives of Saints we have every kind of example of how the Truth Incarnate dwells within and transfigures men. All of them, these images of love, had one thing in common: they were spiritual athletes. They were all ascetics, that is, they excised that which is contrary to nature and exercised in that which was according to nature, so that they were made partakers of divine nature. All of them had this in common: their ascetic life was an expression of their love for Christ. They had no part in the hypocrisy of the legalist or the egotism of the practitioner of sick religiosity.

As Saint John of the Ladder writes:

> *Hypocrisy* is the mother of lying and frequently its cause. Some would argue that hypocrisy is nothing other than a meditation on falsehood, that it is the inventor of falsehood laced with lies.[22]

The Saints eschewed even the slightest measure of hypocrisy for they knew that it would deprive them of the divine "insanity" of communion with God, as Saint Porphyrios describes it:

---

21 I.e., Saints
22 St. John of the Ladder, *The Ladder of Divine Ascent*, Step 12 §6.

Whoever experiences Christ becomes one with Him, with His Church. He experiences a mad delight. This life is different from the life of other people. It is joy, it is light, it is exultation, it is exaltation. This is the life of the Church, the life of the Gospel, the Kingdom of God. "The Kingdom of God is within us." Christ comes within us and we are within Him. This occurs just in the way a piece of iron placed in the fire becomes fire and light; once it is removed from the fire it becomes iron again, black and dark.[23]

Hence, to be a true Orthodox Christian we must go far beyond being a moral person, far beyond religion, to embrace wholeheartedly CHRIST, to be in total love with the Incarnate Truth.

We live in the midst of mass apostasy and many of us are survivors from the shipwreck which is Western civilization. As Saint Justin Popovich, that great lover of the God-man, has said of our age: "Never was there less God in man than today, never less God on earth than today."[24]

The mystery of iniquity which has been at work among the heterodox since the Great Schism has brought us to the point where we are now swimming in a sea of lies: lies about the world, about human nature, human origins, our neighbors, our country, and about God Himself. Perhaps worst of all, we are swimming in a sea of lies about ourselves. We are pushed daily by a narcissistic, nihilistic society to make an idol of ourselves, to live in delusion about who we are, both in terms of our nature and our personal spiritual state. We must seek and attain both *αυτογνωσία* (self-knowledge)

---

23 Elder Porphyrios of Kavsokalyvia, *Wounded by Love* (Limni: Denise Harvey Publisher, 2005), p. 91.

24 Father Justin Popovich, "Last Judgment over God," *Christian Life* (1924), Nos. 7-8.

and *θεογνωσία* (knowing the Hypostatic or Person of Truth, Christ, mysteriologically, experientially).

This brings me to the first step toward forming our children in the love of Truth: seeking and attaining *αυτογνωσία*, or self-knowledge, without which no true spiritual life can be established. As long as we are in darkness about our own selves, our passions, our weaknesses, and the path which leads out of this state of un-truth and delusion, we will be powerless to inspire the love of Truth in our children.

Self-knowledge is obtainable, however, only by coming to *θεογνωσία*, or the knowledge of God. One who sits in the darkness of ignorance of revelation and has yet to see the great Light of Christ appear in his mind's eye, can never truly come to self-knowledge. He can make progress on the path of truth in ideas and creation, but it will forever remain an external and non-salvific, non-transfiguring knowledge of truth, even if his love of it brings him to the door of initiation into the Mystery of Christ, which is the Church.

It is only by becoming one with the fire of divinity in the Holy Mysteries of the Church that one can come to the true knowledge of God and, consequently, to the true knowledge of self. Outside the eucharistic synaxis there is no Church; "there is the rest of humanity being carried to and fro by the prince of this world"[25] to a lesser or greater degree, and "only God can know if there is any salvation."[26]

Saint Gregory Palamas provides us with an essential delineation of the boundaries of truth and of the Church, when he writes:

---

25 John Romanides, "The Ecclesiology of St. Ignatius", accessed December 29, 2022, http://www.romanity.org/htm/rom.11.en.the_ecclesiology_of_st._ignatius_of_antioch.01.htm

26 Ibid.

Ποῖος κλῆρος, ποία μερίς, τίς γνησιότης πρός τήν τοῦ Χριστοῦ ἐκκλησίαν τῷ συνηγόρῳ τοῦ ψεύδους; Ἐκκλησίαν ἥ "στύλος καί ἑδραίωμα τῆς ἀληθείας" κατά Παῦλον ἐστιν, ἥ καί μένει χάριτι Χριστοῦ διηνεκῶς ἀσφαλής καί ἀκράδαντος, ἐστηριγμένη παγίως οἷς ἐπεστήρικται ἡ ἀλήθεια;

Καί γάρ οἱ τῆς Χριστοῦ ἐκκλησίας τῆς ἀληθείας εἰσί· καί οἱ μή τῆς ἀληθείας ὄντες οὐδέ τῆς τοῦ Χριστοῦ ἐκκλησίας εἰσί,

[they are of the Church of Christ who are of the truth, and those who are not of the truth, are not in the Church of Christ]

καί τοσοῦτο μᾶλλον, ὅσον ἄν καί σφῶν αὐτῶν καταψεύδοιντο, ποιμένας καί ἀρχιποιμένας ἱερούς ἑαυτούς καλοῦντες καί ὑπ' ἀλλήλων καλούμενοι· μηδέ γάρ προσώποις τόν Χριστιανισμόν, ἀλλ' ἀληθείᾳ καί ἀκριβείᾳ πίστεως χαρακτηρίζεσθαι μεμνήμεθα.[27]

For St. Gregory it is clear that "being of the truth" refers to the Hypostatic, Incarnate Truth, that is communion in the Mysteries and confession of the Faith, and not simply holding true doctrines or expressing the truth in the realm of ideas. It is BOTH/AND, as always.

So, in so far as we swim in the noetic sea of lies, exchanging and retaining them within us, or are victims of them due to our ignorance and indifference to Truth, we are voluntarily or involuntarily working for the enemy of our salvation, the father of lies, of whom Christ said:

> He was a murderer from the beginning, and abode not in the truth, because there is no truth in him. When he speaketh a lie, he speaketh of his own: for he is a liar, and the father of it.[28]

27 Ἁγίου Γρηγορίου τοῦ Παλαμᾶ. Συγγράμματα Τόμ. Β', σελ. 627
28 John 8:44

On the contrary, the number one characteristic of a Christian is abiding mysteriologically in the Truth, which means speaking the truth as an expression of Him Who dwells within us, having a clear vision of the Truth, and having discernment of the spirits (understanding not only who God is, but who we are, what is going on in us, around us, and in the world of ideas).

Thus, it should be clear that the first and most important step we can take in becoming fountains of "truth-loving" for our children is to go deeper in *αυτογνωσία*—unveiling the truth about ourselves—and *θεογνωσία*—knowing the Hypostatic or Person of Truth, Christ, mysteriologically, experientially.

TRUTH IS MANIFESTED TO US IN TWO DIFFERENT WAYS: ON A VERTICAL PLANE AND ON A HORIZONTAL PLANE

Perhaps it would be helpful to make the following distinction. We could say that Truth is manifested to us in two different ways. One could say that there is Truth with a capital T and truth with a lower case t:

1. Truth with a capital "T" is, of course, Christ Himself
2. Truth with a lower case "t" is that in creation and the realm of ideas.

We could say that the first is Truth on the Vertical Plane and the second is Truth on a Horizontal Plane.

Truth, as a Person, Who is God, is one, and thus both expressions of Truth are essential and inseparable, just like the two bars on a cross.

Saint Justin Popovich writes the following with regard to Truth as a Person:

> "In Christianity truth is not a philosophical concept nor is it a theory, a teaching, or a system, but rather, it is the living theanthropic hypostasis— the historical Jesus Christ (John 14:6). Before Christ men could only conjecture about the Truth since they did not possess it. With Christ as the incarnate divine Logos the eternally complete divine Truth enters into the world. For this reason the Gospel says: *"Truth came by Jesus Christ"* (John 1:17)."[29]

And elsewhere:

> There is only one Truth, one ultimate Truth, for them [the Holy Fathers]: the *Theanthropos*, the Lord Jesus Christ. And the holy ecumenical councils, from first to last, confess, defend, believe, proclaim and watchfully guard one single most precious thing: The *Theanthropos*, the Lord Jesus Christ.[30]

Loving and knowing the first: Truth as a Person, enables one to know the second, truth in the realm of ideas. Loving and knowing the second, truth in ideas, leads one ever closer to the first, Truth as a Person, Christ the Incarnate Logos.

WE LOVE TRUTH AS CHRIST HIMSELF WHEN WE LIVE IN HIM AND ACQUIRE HIS MIND

How do we know if we love Truth as a Person, Christ Himself? We live *in Him*. We acquire His mind.

---

29 Father Justin Popovich, *Orthodox Faith and Life in Christ*, trans. Fr. Asterios Gerostergios, et al. (Belmont, MA: Institute for Byzantine and Modern Greek Studies, 2020), p. 78.

30 Saint Justin Popovich, *The Orthodox Church and Ecumenism*, trans. Benjamin Emmanuel Stanley (Birmingham, AL: Lazarica Press, 2000), p. 52.

St. Paul says the truth of Christ is *in* me, it dwells IN me:

> I am crucified with Christ: nevertheless I live; yet not I, but Christ liveth in me: [ζῶ δὲ οὐκέτι ἐγώ, ζῇ δὲ <u>ἐν ἐμοὶ Χριστός</u>] and the life which I now live in the flesh I live by the faith of the Son of God, who loved me, and gave himself for me.[31]

Likewise, when the Lord speaks of confessing Him before men, He speaks of confessing IN Him:

> πᾶς ὅς ἂν ὁμολογήσῃ <u>ἐν ἐμοὶ</u> ἔμπροσθεν τῶν ἀνθρώπων,[32]

And when He speaks of the Son of Man confessing the confessor of Him in heaven, He speaks of confessing IN him before the angels of God:

> καὶ ὁ υἱὸς τοῦ ἀνθρώπου ὁμολογήσει <u>ἐν αὐτῷ</u> ἔμπροσθεν τῶν ἀγγέλων τοῦ θεοῦ[33]

Whereas, when He speaks of those who deny Him, He simply says, the one who denies Me:

> ὁ δὲ <u>ἀρνησάμενός με</u> ἐνώπιον τῶν ἀνθρώπων ἀπαρνηθήσεται ἐνώπιον τῶν ἀγγέλων τοῦ θεοῦ.[34]

Obviously, then, to confess the Lord is an INTERNAL event, a mystery of theanthropic unity, of the Incarnation, where we love Christ and we acquire Him Who is Truth. As St. Seraphim of Sarov says:

---

31 Galatians 2:20
32 Luke 12:8 (KJV ignores the word "in.")
33 Ibid.
34 Luke 12:9

Acquire the Spirit and a thousand around you will be saved.[35]

But the Holy Spirit is the Spirit of Truth and the Lord Himself said "I am the Truth." Christ said before Pilate:

> To this end was I born, and for this cause came I into the world, that I should bear witness unto the truth. Every one that is of the truth heareth my voice.[36]

Here is the reason for the Incarnation: to witness to the Truth, to witness to Himself; to make God known to man, that he might have COMMUNION with/in God.

Every one that is OF THE TRUTH heareth my voice...

So in this second part is illustrated the inter-relationship of Truth as a Person and truth in our daily lives, in ideas and relationships.

THIS IS KEY: Christ came to set us free by giving us to know the Truth. Thus, being a Christian is NOT defined by becoming a good moral person only, or by performing acts of religion, or by carrying out acts of charity. These are all fruits of a life in Christ, but the defining characteristic of being a Christian is being IN communion with and expressing the Truth, which requires LOVING the Truth, loving Christ. and being *of the truth* in all things. We must love Truth both as a Person and in and in the realm of ideas. If you know Truth as a Person, you will easily know and understand truth in ideas.

---

35 Cf. Archimandrite Lazarus Moore, *An Extraordinary Peace, St. Seraphim, Flame of Sarov*, (Port Townsend, WA: Anaphora Press, 2009), p. 83.

36 John 18:37

THE MIND OF CHRIST IS NOT THE RATIONAL MIND

A sure sign that we love Christ is that we have *acquired His mind*. The Apostle says these extraordinary words: "We have the mind of Christ."

> τίς γὰρ ἔγνω νοῦν κυρίου, ὃς συμβιβάσει αὐτόν; ἡμεῖς δὲ νοῦν χριστοῦ ἔχομεν[37]

Nous not *Dianoia*: So, the "mind" of Christ here refers not to the rational intellect but to the *nous*, which the Apostle elsewhere refers to as "our spirit":

> *The Spirit itself beareth witness with our spirit, that we are the children of God.*[38]

And:

> *For what man knoweth the things of a man, save the spirit of man which is in him?*[39]

Therefore, to "have the mind of Christ" is not an intellectual but a spiritual state in which the eye of the soul, the *nous*, is lucid, communing with the Spirit of God, filled with the Light of God, knowing the reasons of beings and discerning the spirits; being of, and witnessing to, the truth of all things.

It is clear here that the man of the Spirit who has the *Nous* of Christ is not a rationalist. The Apostle refers to a man bereft of the Spirit of God as a "ψυχικὸς ἄνθρωπος," translated as "the natural man":

---

37 I Corinthians 2:16
38 Romans 8:6
39 I Corinthians 2:11

But the natural man *(ψυχικὸς ἄνθρωπος)* receiveth not the things of the Spirit of God: for they are foolishness unto him: neither can he know them, because they are spiritually discerned.[40]

The rationalist does not hear the preaching of repentance, which calls for not a change of his *dianoia* or mind, but a change of his *nous* or spirit:

Μετανοεῖτε γὰρ ἡ βασιλεία τῶν οὐρανῶν ἤγγικεν.[41]

The Lord is not calling us to change the way we think—that will happen, of course—but first of all to change our spiritual stance and orientation, to enlarge our hearts so that the Hypostatic, Incarnate Truth, Who is the Kingdom of Heaven, can establish His Spiritual Reign within.

The rationalist, the *ψυχικὸς ἄνθρωπος*, the category in which most people fall today, does not receive the call to repentance and the things of the Spirit because he has exalted his *διάνοια* or mind above his *νους* or spirit, thus closing off the path to spiritual life. In a word, he does not live in the realm of true life, of reality, and thus has no humility, which is another way of saying does not recognize the truth of things.

Knowing this should help us to better encounter ourselves, our spouses, and most of all our children who are immersed in a sea of rationalism. Countering their refusal to embrace the things of the Spirit with rationalistic arguments succeeds in nothing but to reveal our lack of spiritual

---

40 I Corinthians 2:14
41 "Repent [ye]: for the kingdom of heaven is at hand." Sometimes called the "first words of the Gospel" due to them being the first words both St. John the Forerunner speaks (Matthew 3:2) and the first words the Lord speaks (Matthew 4:17) in the first Gospel account (viz., of St. Matthew).

understanding. As the Apostle said, the things of the Spirit "are foolishness unto them: neither can they know them, because they are spiritually discerned."[42]

Can one be inspired to nail the rational man to the Cross of Love when he has supplanted the Crucified One with himself? If our children do not first taste of the fruits of the love of Truth, offered lovingly to them at our spiritual table, how can they be expected or inspired to commend themselves and their whole life unto Christ our God? The rationalist is insecure and we are expecting him to step off a cliff and trust that which his mind's eye has yet to discern: the spiritual realm. There is a security and peace, false and delusional though it be, in the "natural man's" clinging to earthly life.

THE MIND OF CHRIST IS SPEAKING AND WITNESSING TO THE TRUTH

To have the mind of Christ, then, one will be speaking and witnessing to the Truth, able to discern the spirits. It is here that, as Fr. Seraphim Rose once wrote, the difference between Orthodoxy and heterodoxy is most apparent, namely, that the Orthodox Church (in Her Saints) is able to discern the spirits. This discernment of the methods of the fallen spirits is, in fact, a requirement in the formation of Christology and Ecclesiology. As the Evangelist John writes, *"For this purpose the Son of God was manifested, that he might destroy the works of the devil."*[43]

Insomuch, therefore, as one has reoriented his spirit to receive the Dayspring of the Orient, and has been purified from the passions and illumined by the Spirit of God,

---

42 I Corinthians 2:14
43 1 John 3:8

so much so is his spiritual vision open and discernment acquired. This great gift of discernment—separating the wheat from the chaff, the lie from the truth—presupposes initiation into the death, resurrection and life of Christ which is lived within His Body, the Church. That few Orthodox Christians possess a good measure of this gift is a testament to the inroads of the spirit of antichrist, which, by another name, is secularism. The end of the worldly spirit is the denial of the theanthropic nature of the Christ and His Body, "the hour of temptation, which shall come upon all the world, to try them that dwell upon the earth"[44] before the ascent of the man of iniquity, the Antichrist. This temptation is coming upon the world primarily through the spread of the ecclesiological heresy known as ecumenism.

The dearth of the discernment among men is a sign of the times, to be sure, but it is also an opportunity for all Orthodox Christians to speak truth in the realm of ideas, in society, and lead many toward Truth as a Person, to Christ Himself. Our children rejoice in seeing their parents love the Truth more than security, risking the *status quo* for the *statu patriae*, the heavenly state.

Saint Paisios of the Holy Mountain said:

> In the old days, if a believer worried about the state of the world, he was thought not to be right in the head and was destined for confinement in the Tower.[45] Today it's just the opposite; a believer is destined for confinement in the Tower if he's not concerned for and doesn't feel pain over the prevailing conditions in the world.[46]

---

44 Revelation 3:10
45 A tall defensive structure built into the monasteries of the Holy Mountain and used to ward off pirates.
46 St. Paisios the Athonite, *Spiritual Counsels II: Spiritual Awakening*,

Two points:

1. Today's leaders are out to destroy the Church, the family, the youth. You cannot trust them, you cannot leave matters to them as if they are benevolent and working for our good.
2. Saint Paisios sees witnessing to truth in society as a form of confession of our faith in Christ, of an expression of our love.

Elsewhere he says the following:

> We want others to pull the chestnuts out of the fire so that we can have our peace of mind. This indicates a lack of love. Then man begins to act out of self-interest. This is why we see an all-too-familiar spirit today: 'Get to know so-and-so because he will then speak well of you. Be on good terms with so-and-so and he will not speak badly of you, and so forth. After all, we must not be taken for fools, we must not become victims.' Another person remains indifferent and does not speak up. 'I do not speak out,' he says, 'so that I won't be written up in the newspapers.' In other words, most people are completely indifferent.[47]

Notice here that the elder equates silence before iniquity in society as lack of love. How different that is from the prevailing view of love in our society, which speaks of love only in romantic or fleshly terms (and they usually mean self-love).

(Souroti: Holy Monastery "Evangelist John the Theologian," 2014), p. 24. [Translated from the Greek.]

47 Ibid. pp. 40-41. [Translated from the Greek.]

Here love means love of the brethren, love of the truth, and sacrifice for them and for Christ.

This means that our love of Christ, of Truth, of a Person, cannot mean that we are indifferent to truth in ideas and actions, in society. Just the *opposite* is the case. When we are in pain and suffer for the lack of truth in society, then we are approaching Truth as Person.

The lover of Truth as a Person, of our Lord, is all the more concerned with truth in the realm of ideas, with the fate of his brethren mired in the muck of delusion all the more ready to speak a *prophetic* word to the world.

We cannot be indifferent to questions of our day, to the questions of truth on the horizontal plane, and think that we love *Truth* as a Person, Christ Himself.

The words of the Apostle John are clear:

> *If a man say, I love God, and hateth his brother, he is a liar: for he that loveth not his brother whom he hath seen, how can he love God whom he hath not seen?*[48]

So, just as one cannot claim to love his brother when he stands indifferent to him as he stands hungry or naked, so too, and even much more, one cannot claim to love his brother and yet be indifferent to him as he is fed lies and is bereft of the Truth.

Christ Himself said that He was sent:

> *"to preach deliverance to the captives, and recovering of sight to the blind, to set at liberty them that are bruised."*[49]

Here He is clearly not speaking only about political liberties; He is speaking primarily about spiritual liberation.

---

48 I John 4:20
49 Luke 4:18; Isaiah 61:1

If we are to be His disciples, and He is to dwell within us, then we must follow Him in this deliverance from spiritual captivity.

Everywhere people are held captive today in the realm of ideas, blind to the truth, and enslaved. This slavery, this blindness, on the horizontal plane, makes it nearly impossible for them to know truth on vertical plane—to draw near to Christ.

The Church—you and I—must stand and speak truth to them with boldness and in a prophetic way. If the Church ceases to be prophetic in this world, it ceases to carry out its mission; ceases to be the Church and loses its ring of authenticity, which is most precious to the children.

This boldness will inevitably mean—as Saint Paisios says—that many will feel uneasy, whether among the believers or the heterodox, but this is a "good uneasiness." This is a *necessary*, a *beneficial* uneasiness, which awakens the conscience and brings the soul to salvific knowledge. For many of our children this is going to be the first step on the path of loving the truth. It will be painful but it will be salvific.

In speaking of the last times, the Apostle Paul gives us the very instructive and revealing teaching to guide us. He says:

> *The spirit of delusion works with all deceivableness of unrighteousness in them that perish; because they received not the love of Truth, that they might be saved.*[50]

Clearly, the Apostle has the love of truth as the criterion of salvation, of our salvation, in the Church. In the kingdom of lies, in which we all live today, the love of truth is the key to heaven.

---

50 I Thessalonians 2:10

Skete in a cave in Tsagarada of Pelion
(known as the "Hidden School").

Saints Gregory the Theologian, John Chrysostom, and Basil the Great

CHAPTER III

On the Patristic and "Post-Patristic" View of Education and Salvation

Lecture delivered at the
Orthodox Homeschool Conference: "Have Faith"
April 19-22, 2018
St. Nicholas Ranch, Dunlap, CA

Venerable Fathers, Esteemed Colleagues, Brothers and Sisters, Christ is Risen!

It is an honor and a joy to join you, my fellow Orthodox home-schoolers, here today in this beautiful retreat center and near the Life-Giving Monastery of the Theotokos the Life-Giving Spring. I would like to thank the Antiochian Archdiocese Department of Homeschooling and Fr. Noah Bushelli, as well as the St. Kosmas Orthodox Homeschool association and Christine Hall, for the invitation to speak to you today.

THE MEANING OF THE "POST-PATRISTIC" VIEW AND HOW IT HAS AFFECTED HOMESCHOOLING

The title of my talk is, most likely, a little disorienting for many of you. I am sure you all know what patristic means, but what does "post-patristic" mean? The term itself is used in the sense of relativism, partial or total questioning, re-evaluation, a new reading, or even the transcendence of the thought of the Fathers of the Church.

When we speak of post-Patristic theology or theologians this refers to a contemporary movement among a small but unfortunately growing segment of academic theologians, mainly in Greece and America, who are calling on the Church to, among much else, "move beyond the fathers" of the Church, to "reinterpret our dogmatic teaching," and to consider all heterodox Christians as a part of the One Church.[51]

According to Professor Demetrios Tselengides:

> "This movement of so-called "post-Patristic" theologians which has appeared in recent years, is organically embedded in [today's] broader, secularized, theological climate, and particularly in the spirit of Ecumenism itself... Certainly, this movement also has Protestant influences, which are particularly clear in the scientific nature of the attitude of the "post-patristic" theologians to the theological teaching of the Holy Fathers."[52]

---

51 See the Letter of Metropolitan Paul of Glyfadas who succinctly presents the matter, here: https://www.johnsanidopoulos.com/2012/03/contextual-or-post-patristic-theology.html

52 Demetrios Tselengidis, "Post-Patristic or Neo-Barlaamite Theology", accessed April 30, 2024, http://orthodox-voice.blogspot.nl/2013/05/patristic-theology-and-post-patristic.html

The two most basic presuppositions which "post-patristic" theology/theologians ignore are:

1. That the experience of spiritual life in Christ in the Church is the foundational presupposition of theologizing in an Orthodox and delusion-free manner.

2. Orthodox and delusion-free theology is only produced by those who have been cleansed of the impurity of their passions and, moreover, those who have been enlightened by the uncreated rays of divinizing grace.

When holiness or even Orthodox theological methodology of "following the holy Fathers" is set aside, "the adoption of theological reflection and speculation is inevitable."[53] Here is where the post-patristic theologians and the infamous Barlaam of Calabria converge "in a theology which is anthropocentric and has as its criterion self-validating reason."[54]

Let us refresh our memory a bit about Barlaam and his theology. The patrologist Panagiotis Chrestou explains:

> "Barlaam bore the influence of the Renaissance, which began to rise at this time, and he considered the revelation of God to be static, limited to biblical times, and he denied that it existed in the current life of the Church, namely the experience of the monks. At the same time, he sought a new authenticity, outside of Christianity, personified by the great philosophers of ancient times.

---

53 Ibid.
54 Ibid.

He thus explained the revelation of God based on Greek philosophy and not on the basis of the hesychastic tradition, which survived vibrantly in the Eastern Christian Roman Empire, especially Mount Athos. This is the reason why Barlaam was in opposition to Athonite monasticism, as it was expressed by Saint Gregory Palamas."[55]

Just as Barlaam and his followers doubted the uncreated nature of the divine light and divine grace, so too contemporary "post-patristic" theologians effectively ignore the uncreated and, therefore, enduring character of the sanctity and teaching of the God-bearing Fathers, whom they attempt to replace, as regards teaching, by producing their own original theology. This is not a battle against the Fathers, of an external nature, but in essence a battle against God, because what makes the Fathers of the Church really Fathers is their uncreated sanctity, which, indirectly but to all intents and purposes, these theologians set aside and cancel out with their "post-Patristic" theology.

You are probably all wondering, that is all fine and good, but what does it have to do with homeschooling our children? Allow me to connect the dots.

Two main characteristics of Barlaamism that we see re-emerging today are:

- The interpretation of Holy Scripture based on philosophical and dialectic reasoning as well as thoughtful analysis and not on the living hesychastic experience.

---

[55] Metropolitan Hierotheos (Vlachos), "Barlaamism in Contemporary Theology", accessed April 30, 2024, https://www.johnsanidopoulos.com/2014/10/barlaamism-in-contemporary-theology-1.html

- The view that theology, or the knowledge of God, is the objective experience of the senses, the imagination and logical processes, and not the fruit of personal experience, which is how the hesychast monks experienced it.

This idea that one can make progress on the path of salvation, or that it is even obtained through the ascent of the *rational* intellect to the knowledge *about* God, is ever so slightly creeping into Orthodox homeschooling rhetoric, most surely unbeknownst to most.

Allow me to give you a few examples:

1. The direct association of education, study and reflection, with *theosis*, as if the former were means to the latter.
2. The idea that *the goal* of our reading and writing and rhetoric is *theosis*, again implying the one leads to the other.
3. The putting of the Holy Tradition of the Fathers on equal footing with the tradition of Ancient Greece, and claiming that both can help train us to overcome the passions.
4. And, finally, the idea that education is itself a means by which we can overcome the passions, as opposed to a *preparatory* step, much like, as the Apostle Paul writes, "the law was our schoolmaster *to bring us* unto Christ, that we might be justified by faith, after which *we are no longer under a schoolmaster.*" (Gal 3:24)

Keep these four examples in mind as we now turn to look at the approach of the Holy Fathers to Classical Education.

THE FATHERS OF THE CHURCH AND CLASSICAL EDUCATION

The Fathers of the Church are today often held up as great examples of the indispensability of including pagan, classical literature in Christian education. Some Fathers were well versed in classical literature and philosophy, perhaps as few of their contemporaries. Of this, no one can doubt.

Did, however, the great hierarchs of the Church become great theologians because of their classical education? Or, were their years spent in reading pagan philosophy and literature a prerequisite to become great theologians?

If one remembers the famous patristic saying, "If you are a theologian you truly pray. If you truly pray you are a theologian,"[56] then the answer is apparent. A better question is: did the Great Hierarchs use their pagan education *as a tool* in their pastoral and apologetic work for the upbuilding of the Church? The answer to this is, of course, yes.

The Fathers of that age were shepherds of their rational flocks and indeed the entire Church at a time of great change, straddling, as it were, the outgoing pagan world and the rising Christian empire. Their pastoral task was to speak of heavenly truths to earth-bound wise-men in terms and a language which they understood. In order to understand their engagement with what we now call the "classical world" and its philosophy and mythology, it is crucial always to have this *pastoral context* in mind. In particular, one must understand that they were first of all approaching pagan, non-Christian culture and literature *kat'oikonomia* or according to pastoral condescension and not in search of the knowledge of God. Their employment (and transformation) of philosophical terms and ideas was not an end in itself but

---

56 Evagrius Ponticus, *Chapters on Prayer*, chapter 60.

chiefly a means by which to bring uninitiated men to *"the full knowledge of the truth."*[57]

A. Two Types of Wisdom

In the writings of the Three Hierarchs, but also in the epistles of the Apostles Paul and James, and indeed the entire patristic tradition, there are two types of wisdom:

- ἄνωθεν: from above (or divine and true) and
- θύραθεν: from without (or human and worldly)

Each type of wisdom has limits as to its development, its aims, and the means by which it is acquired.[58]

The wisdom which comes from above (ἄνωθεν), from God, by revelation, is obtained by the enlightenment of the Holy Spirit. It is not limited, as is human knowledge. God Himself is revealed in His divine energies (actions). His mysterious presence in creation is inscrutable. It cannot be subjected to human inspection and proof. Man either receives God's mysteries with faith (trust), and sees that "God is good," or he rejects them.

The ἄνωθεν wisdom leads man to salvation, to regeneration, to taking man from the image to the likeness of God, to his perfection. Divine wisdom makes the passionate, impassive; the earthly, heavenly; the mindless, Godly-minded; the mortal, immortal.

The wisdom which comes from men, or θύραθεν, is obtained by human means, with study and reflection. Within

---

57 II Timothy 3:7
58 Μητροπολίτη Καισαριανῆς, Βύρωνος καί Ὑμηττοῦ, Δανιήλ, "Η διπλή γνώση: ἄνωθεν καί θύραθεν σοφία," http://www.imkby.gr/index.php/δημοκρατια/1045-ή- διπλή-γνώση-ἄνωθεν-καί-θύραθεν-σοφία-1-ημ-δημοσίευσης-31-1-2015

human (θύραθεν) wisdom, the mind is taught to judge, to meditate upon, to follow principles and human rules of logic, in order to examine the earthly, the created. It cannot, however, thereby judge and examine that which is from above, and that which is uncreated.

The following passage from the Apostle Paul's epistle to the Corinthians is very enlightening for us in our examination of the two wisdoms:

> "Howbeit we speak wisdom among them that are perfect: yet not the wisdom of this world, nor of the princes of this world, that come to nought: But we speak the wisdom of God in a mystery, *even* the hidden *wisdom*, which God ordained before the world unto our glory: Which none of the princes of this world knew: for had they known *it*, they would not have crucified the Lord of glory. But as it is written, Eye hath not seen, nor ear heard, neither have entered into the heart of man, the things which God hath prepared for them that love him. But God hath revealed them unto us by his Spirit: for the Spirit searcheth all things, yea, the deep things of God. For what man knoweth the things of a man, save the spirit of man which is in him? even so the things of God knoweth no man, but the Spirit of God. Now we have received, not the spirit of the world, but the spirit which is of God; that we might know the things that are freely given to us of God. Which things also we speak, not in the words which man's wisdom teacheth, but which the Holy Ghost teacheth; comparing spiritual things with spiritual. But the natural man receiveth not the things of the Spirit of God: for they are foolishness unto him: neither can he know them, because they are spiritually-discerned. But he

that is spiritual judgeth all things, yet he himself is judged of no man. For who hath known the mind of the Lord, that he may instruct him? But we have the mind of Christ"[59]

Hence, this θύραθεν or worldly wisdom is not necessary for salvation and must not become an end in itself. Contrast this with the thinking of Barlaam, as summarized by Metropolitan Hierotheos Vlachos:

> "Barlaam gives priority to "outer wisdom" or philosophy, which even monks should seek, because only through human wisdom can we achieve dispassion, to approach perfection and sanctification. This is because he considers Greek education to be a gift from God similar to the revelation given to the Prophets and Apostles."[60]

If worldly wisdom cannot be claimed as a means to salvation, it can, however, cooperate with and assist the heaven-sent (ἄνωθεν) wisdom toward the supreme aim of our salvation. It should be seen as a tool, and its value, then, lies in its use and it depends upon the proper perspective and disposition of the one employing it, whether or not he has respect for the things of God, according to the psalmist, "The fear of the LORD is the beginning of wisdom."[61]

---

59 I Corinthians 2:6–16
60 Metropolitan Hierotheos (Vlachos), "Barlaamism in Contemporary Theology", accessed April 30, 2024, https://www.johnsanidopoulos.com/2014/10/barlaamism-in-contemporary-theology-2.html
61 Psalm 110:10 LXX

B. St. Basil the Great and His Example

In this perspective, then, we can see that the Holy Fathers' use of the terms and ideas put forward by the human wisdom of their day was *a pastoral tool, a pastoral condescension*—with full respect, but also full knowledge of the limits of that wisdom.

When classical educators look for patristic support for finding God through pagan literature, they cite first and almost exclusively St. Basil the Great. In his famous "Address to Young Men on the Right Use of Greek Literature"[62] the Saint wrote the following:

> "Now, then, altogether after the manner of bees must we use these writings, for the bees do not visit all the flowers without discrimination, nor indeed do they seek to carry away entirely those upon which they light, but rather, having taken so much as is adapted to their needs, they let the rest go. So we, if wise, shall take from heathen books whatever befits us and is allied to the truth, and shall pass over the rest. And just as in culling roses we avoid the thorns, from such writings as these we will gather everything useful, and guard against the noxious."[63]

First of all, it is apparent here that far from rushing indiscriminately, headlong into pagan literature the Saint is selectively lighting on that which is redeemable, salvaging

---

62 St. Basil the Great, "Address to Young Men on the Right Use of Greek Literature," in English translation in Frederick Morgan Padelford, , *Essays on the Study and Use of Poetry by Plutarch and Basil the Great*, Yale Studies in English 15 (1902) pp. 99-120. (Also available online: https://www.tertullian.org/fathers/basil_litterature01.htm)

63 Ibid.

what he can from the noxious writings of "natural men" (I Cor. 6:14-16).

Secondly, although it is not debated that St. Basil knew classical Greek literature as a whole very well, it needs to be said his education was obtained long before his initiation into Christ and it was a providential preparation and apologetical tool to better wield the ultimate weapon, the Truth revealed in Christ and manifest in the Holy Scriptures.

What is often overlooked, however, in this discussion is that the Fathers had little choice in the matter. In the fourth century the mainstream education curriculum was based on Ancient Greek literature and thus the youths' encounter with it, including mythology and other fiction, was a given. St. Basil had no choice *but to prepare* young people for the texts that they were going to encounter.

We need to remember that St. Basil and his friend, St. Gregory the Theologian, although raised in Christian homes, had undergone this education *before being baptized* and although both were quite familiar with pagan myths, they harshly ridiculed them.[64] Reading pagan fiction (mythology) was, then, not a choice made in adulthood, post baptism.

St. Basil himself in Epistle 223[65] writes that he wept many tears for the days of his adolescence which he had spent in vain, studying philosophy, the "wisdom of this world that God made foolish."[66] It is only logical to assume that what he writes concerning philosophy applies much more to mythology (or fiction):

> Much time had I spent in vanity, and had wasted nearly all my youth in the vain labour which I

---

64 See: St. Gregory's works *Contra Julianum Imperatorem* - Κατά Ἰουλιανοῦ Βασιλέως στηλιτευτικοὶ *1 & 2*.

65 PG 32, 824AB

66 I Corinthians 1: 20

underwent in acquiring the wisdom made foolish by God (cf. I Cor. 1:20). Then once upon a time, like a man roused from deep sleep, I turned my eyes to the marvellous light of the truth of the Gospel, and I perceived the uselessness of "the wisdom of the princes of this world, that come to naught" (I Cor. 2:6). I wept many tears over my miserable life and I prayed that guidance might be vouchsafed me to admit me to the doctrines of true religion. First of all was I minded to make some mending of my ways, long perverted as they were by my intimacy with wicked men. Then I read the Gospel, and I saw there that a great means of reaching perfection was the selling of one's goods, the sharing them with the poor, the giving up of all care for this life, and the refusal to allow the soul to be turned by any sympathy to things of earth. And I prayed that I might find some one of the brethren who had chosen this way of life, that with him I might cross life's short and troubled strait. And many did I find in Alexandria, and many in the rest of Egypt, and others in Palestine, and in Cœle Syria, and in Mesopotamia. I admired their continence in living, and their endurance in toil; I was amazed at their persistency in prayer, and at their triumphing over sleep; subdued by no natural necessity, ever keeping their souls' purpose high and free, in hunger, in thirst, in cold, in nakedness (cf. II Cor. 11:27) they never yielded to the body; they were never willing to waste attention on it; always, as though living in a flesh that was not theirs, they showed in very deed what it is to sojourn for a while in this life, and what to have one's citizenship and home in heaven. All this moved my admiration. I called these men's lives blessed, in that they did in deed show that they "bear about in their body the dying of Jesus" (II Cor. 4:10). And I prayed that I, too, as far as in me lay, might imitate them.[67]

What the Saint describes here is essentially his inner, spiritual conversion and coming to the knowledge of the truth of life in Christ, a process which led away from the vanity of the worldly wisdom of "natural men" to the wisdom from above found in the ascetics and under the direction of a spiritual father.

THE DIACHRONIC WITNESS OF THE FATHERS ON THE SUPERIORITY OF CHRISTIAN WISDOM

Throughout the history of the Church the stance of the Saints has been consistent: they commend the study of classical learning, with discernment, but give clear precedence to Christian wisdom. The example of St. Photios the Great is indicative:

While supporting classical learning alongside of spiritual formation St. Photios advises:

> Give yourself over to our own noble muses too, seeing that these differ from those of the pagans as much as freemen differ from slaves and as much as truth differs from flattery.... True, divine gladness, that which is proper to man... Springs from the Holy Scriptures and our zealous study of them.[68]

---

67 St. Basil of Caesarea, Letter 223, Against Eustathius of Sebasteia, accessed April 30, 2024, https://www.newadvent.org/fathers/3202223.htm

68 St. Photios the Great. *Amphilochios.* Question 107. See: Protopresbyter Theodore Zisis, *Following the Holy Fathers* (Columbia: New Rome Press, 2017), p. 186.

There is a clear hierarchy of things pertaining both to man's make-up and to his education and formation. It is no accident that the Lord chose fishermen rather than Pharisees as his disciples, thus pointing to the superiority of His grace over the power of the human mind. St. Photios, responding to a question concerning how the illiterate Apostles managed to overcome pagan rhetoric, writes:

> "If the mind is greater than the written word, and divine grace is—by an incomprehensible measure—greater than the mind, then you ought not be at all surprised if the Apostles, who possessed the greater [mind] and the greatest [divine grace] completely overwhelmed those—I mean, the rhetors and the philosophers—who showed great arrogance on account of their possession of the least."[69]

One needs to always have this hierarchy in mind, both when reading the Scriptures and Fathers and teaching their children, otherwise he will be misled into believing that, unlike the Holy Apostles, the Great Hierarchs were "great" because of their worldly education and not their spiritual initiation.

Another example brought forth by St. Photios to illustrate this hierarchy and the pastoral condescension of the Saints is the stance of the Apostle Paul when he spoke to the pagans in Athens concerning the altar of an unknown god.[70] Fr. Theodore Zisis summarizes St. Photios the Great's commentary on this as follows:

> "The Apostle Paul's use of classical idioms… does not mean that he somehow abandoned his basic

---

69 Ibid.
70 Acts 17:23

position that the truth must be built upon spiritual realities alone 'comparing spiritual things with spiritual,' for it is indeed he who calls 'the Mosaic law itself chaff, when compared to the supreme wisdom of Christ.' It would be truly unworthy of Paul's divine illumination were he to 'compose truth from myths.' On the contrary, here he is simply condescending to the Athenians' weakness, to their spiritual infancy, which would not allow them to see the truth directly, thereby pedagogically preparing them so that the truth's rays might illumine their minds."[71]

COMING TO THE KNOWLEDGE (*EPIGNOSIS*) OF THE TRUTH

The Fathers' primary task, then, as shepherds and catechists was not simply to teach, much less to inform, but rather to initiate a proud and rationalist world into the Mystery of the Gospel. This is the heart of the work of the catechist or teacher: to initiate his disciple into the event of Pentecost. In fact, the Greek word for catechism, "*κατήχηση*," is formed from the event of Pentecost, when a sound (*ἦχος*) came down (*κάτω*) from heaven.

The aim of the Fathers' pastoral work was not one of moral improvement or rational development but of supra-rational communion with the Holy Trinity, which presupposes repentance, purification and initiation. To paraphrase the Apostle of Love, "that which they had seen and heard from the beginning," that of which they had *επίγνωσης*, or first-hand, experiential knowledge, that they

---

71 St. Photios the Great. *Amphilochios*. Question 107. See: Protopresbyter Theodore Zisis, *Following the Holy Fathers* (Columbia, MO: New Rome Press, 2017), p. 186.

declared unto the fourth century pagan world, "that they may also have communion" with them and the Holy Trinity. The Holy Fathers did not believe that salvation was simply a matter of obtaining γνώσης (knowledge), but, rather, επίγνωσης, experiential knowledge of God Himself, of His uncreated energies, which meant first of all entry into the Church and initiation into the life in Christ. This initiation was a process of purification and illumination, of divesting oneself of the passions and heretical ideas of the rationalists and investing oneself with the mind of Christ and Orthodox *phronema* or mindset; of putting off the old man of sin and death and putting on the resurrected and ascended humanity of Christ.

Enlightenment for the Holy Fathers did not chiefly mean the acquiring of knowledge ABOUT God, ABOUT the truth in terms of ideas—although this can be helpful and an important preparatory step—but rather all learning was meant to lead *to personal, experiential knowledge* of the Truth Incarnate. They undoubtedly encountered in their day that which the Apostle Paul describes as a characteristic of the last days, namely, men who had "the form of piety" but denied "the power thereof," who are "always learning" but "never able to come to a full knowledge (επίγνωσης) of the truth."[72]

This is a characteristic of the heretical man: having lost the ethos or way of life he innovates and shipwrecks with regard to the dogma or truth of Christ. Or vice-versa: having ignored or devalued the dogmas of the Church as the basis of spiritual life, he soon falls into a worldly, grace-obstructing way of life.[73]

72   II Timothy 3:5,7
73   Τσελεγγίδης. Δημήτριος, "Δόγμα και ζωή, μία αδιάρρηκτη συνύπαρξη", Accessed April 29, 2024, http://www.impantokratoros.gr/67DEFBCF.el.aspx

Thus, given the ever-imminent threat of heresy, much of the Fathers' pastoral and catechetical work consisted of the struggle against heresy and heretically-minded men. The heretics used worldly philosophy to logically examine and pronounce upon the things of God which surpassed logic—and they did this without the necessary pre-requisite of experience. Our Saints fought heresy at its root, stressing in word and deed that dogmatic Truth and the Way or Ethos of Christ are inseparable, two sides of the same coin; that there is no possibility for the autonomy of one from the other; and that the loss of one is the loss of the whole.

As St. John Chrysostom wrote:

> "There is no benefit from a pure life when one professes heretical dogma and, likewise, the opposite is true: right dogma is of no benefit when one leads a corrupt life."
>
> ["Οὐδέν ὄφελος βίου καθαροῦ, δογμάτων διεφθαρμένων, ὥσπερ οὐδέ τοὐναντίον, δογμάτων ὑγιῶν, ἐάν ὁ βίος ᾖ διεφθαρμένος"][74]

And elsewhere:

> "Let us not think that holding the faith alone is sufficient for salvation, if we do not also show forth a pure life."
>
> [Μηδέ νομίζωμεν ἀρκεῖν ἡμῖν πρός σωτηρίαν τήν πίστιν, ἐάν μή βίον ἐπιδειζώμεθα καθαρόν.][75]

For him who has a corrupt life it is a matter of time that he will adopt heretical dogmas. Although we are not to concern ourselves with the corrupt lives of others, we *are* called to examine the dogma and the faith of

---

74 P.G. 53,31 καί P.G. 59, 369

75 P.G. 59, 77

others—*including bishops*—as our Holy Fathers instruct us. We judge on the basis of that which we have all inherited, both in our Chrismation and in the Holy Tradition.

In Church life today we observe the tragic consequences when clergy and laity ignore the inseparable relation of faith and life, both with the temptation on the left and that on the right. Whether one has shipwrecked in terms of faith or in terms of life, it matters little to the enemy of our salvation. His aim is to remove us from the full life of the Church, to deprive us of the grace of God and make us into the "world." Whether you exit the Church on the right or the left, he cares not—so long as you exit, so long as you are removed from the Mystery and Mysteries.

The Work of Initiating our Children into the Mystery

There is a great pitfall that we can all slip into when following (as we are often encouraged to do) not the illumined and deified (of which there are few) but the academic "experts." Namely, it is to make the goal of our education μάθηση (fact learning) as opposed to επίγνωσης (experiential knowledge) and μύηση (initiation). The focus of our work becomes producing intellectuals and academics, quite knowledgeable about many things, no doubt, but not initiated into the Mystery.

When the spiritual and intellectual center of our education moves from the altar to the podium, or from the Gospel book to the text book, or from the prayer[76] to social work, then we have acquired the "form of piety" without "the power thereof." In such a case, the "επίγνωσης of the truth"—the experience of, communion with, Christ—will

---

76 I.e., the Jesus Prayer

remain something sought for but never actualized. And then the fearful words of our Lord will be applied:

> "*Ye are the salt of the earth: but if the salt hath lost his savour, wherewith shall it be salted? it is thenceforth good for nothing, but to be cast out, and to be trodden under foot of men.*" (Matt. 5:13)

One cause of falling into this tragic error is the loss of discernment in how to "hierarchize," or prioritize spiritual matters. This error, in turn, is caused by the encroachment of the worldly spirit due to alienation from the ascetic life as the presupposition of participation in the Mystery and Mysteries of Christ.

If we truly wish to be "followers of the Holy Fathers," to be Orthodox in practice, it is necessary that we also be following them in the presuppositions of their dogmatic teaching, which is, namely, their life in the Holy Spirit, the pre-requisite of which is purification from the passions and enlightenment of the intellect through God's divinizing grace. This purification from the passions is considered of greater importance than theology itself by the great Theologian himself, St. Gregory, for only then can the intellect of man truly come to know God *by participation in Him*.

In this context, we sadly observe that our contemporary academic theology has (with a few notable exceptions) not followed Patristic theology. The reason for this appears to be because it has been deeply affected by the secularized, heterodox theological environment in the West. In particular, this refers to their theological methodology and mistaken theological presuppositions.

Western heterodox theological methodology is mainly based upon reductive and abstract functioning of the intellect, which is, in the final analysis, autonomous from God. Thus, in the West, dogmas were mainly considered to be theological ideas which are conceived in the mind without any particular relation to the life of the one expressing it. On the contrary, Orthodox theological methodology is experiential, characterized by living knowledge of God which is actualized within the Church, the communion of *theosis*.

Therefore, it should be clear why the Holy Fathers, although valuing θύραθεν (human wisdom), knew its proper place and did not allow it to supplant the central place which ἄνωθεν (divine wisdom) occupies, and while engaging in theological discourse they never lost sight of the spiritual presuppositions.

Today, one observes generally that there is confusion or ignorance as to the hierarchy of things in spiritual and intellectual life, including in home education. In order for everything to ultimately serve our ascent, however, it is essential that the hierarchy of things is maintained.

THE USE OF ΘΥΡΑΘΕΝ PHILOSOPHY IN CHRISTIAN EDUCATION TODAY

What does all of this mean for us today? Is it good for Orthodox children to study the ancient philosophers and read pagan literature, or not? Is there any benefit for Orthodox children? Is there any harm in it?

One possible answer, abrupt as it is, was given by St. Gregory of Nyssa, who was no stranger to worldly wisdom. He said: "Secular [or worldly] education, in very truth, is infertile, always in labor, and never giving life to its offspring."[77]

This is not to say that St. Gregory did not make use of it. As we saw above, the Fathers used it as a tool in their work of upbuilding the Church. The question, then, is not primarily should Orthodox children approach worldly

---

77 St. Gregory of Nyssa, *De Vita Moysis*, II, 36.

wisdom in search of *the Light*, as if they do not have Him, but is this worldly wisdom *useful?* Is it a *means* to the *end* (or aim) of our life?

The answer to these questions is manifest when we answer another, more basic question: what is the true aim of our Christian life? On this, St. Seraphim of Sarov has this to say:

> "Prayer, fasting, vigil and all other Christian practices, however good they may be in themselves, do not constitute the aim of our Christian life, although they serve as the indispensable means of reaching this end. The true aim of our Christian life consists in the acquisition of the Holy Spirit of God."[78]

The only Good *per se*, then, is the acquisition of the Holy Spirit. Among the means to reaching this end one could include spiritual study, of course, but is it good to study θύραθεν philosophy and literature? It could be "good" contingent upon a positive response to this question: does it lead one to the acquisition of the Holy Spirit?[79]

Within the Orthodox spirit and ethos the pursuit of the *telos*, the end, is ultimately free of the *deon*, or "duty" or "rules." This is most apparent in the lives of the "fools-for-Christ." However, the freedom of holiness presupposes purification from the passions. A salvific use of freedom has as its *sine qua non* freedom from the passions, usually obtained after long ascetic struggle. For most of us, such freedom is

---

78 Trans. Hieromonk Seraphim (Rose), *Little Russian Philokalia, Vol.1: St Seraphim*, 4th ed. (Platina, CA: St Herman of Alaska Brotherhood, 1996), p.79.

79 With respect to these and subsequent reflections, I am indebted to Deacon Aaron Taylor for his study, *Reading Imaginative Literature: A Study in Orthodox Moral Theology.*

still to come, after we learn obedience to Christ in His Body and under the direction of an experienced spiritual father.

What does this imply for the education of our children and the use of θύραθεν wisdom? In practice it means we make of it *selective use for particularly suited children in high school of late high school age.* Why? For the same reason that it is unwise to expose a newly planted tree to high winds and rain without it first putting down roots: it will most likely be uprooted. As homeschooling parents, the truth of this should be obvious to all of us, for on this same basis we also decided not to send our young souls into the storm of public schools.

Putting down roots here means a thorough grounding in the realism of the Holy Scriptures and Lives of the Saints, and years living within the grace of God and under the shelter of obedience to a spiritual father. Thus, when they are exposed to the gusts of the "natural man's" philosophy and the rain of idolatrous fancy they will weather the storm and be the better for it.

Even this discerning use of worldly wisdom and pagan literature is not a *necessity*, nor recommended for some. As we saw above, even St. Basil the Great, who had the task to guide young men through the wilderness of pagan literature, realized late in life that there was no need *for him* to do it *for his salvation*. The narrow path is winding, to be sure, but one does not *need* to pass through Athens to reach Jerusalem. If some do, for whatever historical or pastoral or intellectual reason, that is another matter, and it may be, as it was in St. Basil's case, providential and ultimately for the upbuilding of the Church.

Here, someone might respond: not everything *has to* serve the aim of the acquisition of the Holy Spirit, *does it*? How about just fulfilling the need for students to develop intellectually, read, write and speak well, become good citizens, function in society, etc.?

Undoubtedly, there is need of developing these skills and gifts. That is why, ultimately, the particulars of the decision belong to the parents, who will decide on a case-by-case basis when and how much of the wisdom offered for life in this world is necessary and beneficial for their children's mental and educational development.[80]

In the process of discernment, however, let them not acquiesce to the proud thought that ALL of my children must be well-versed in the wisdom of this world in order to go to college. Or, ALL of my children must become professionals or teachers. This thought, inspired from the demon of pride on the right, has led many an innocent soul into the fire of fornication and darkness of disbelief. Beyond the sad reality of the university today, the system of which has been rightly labeled the *Gulag Archipelago* of America, this is an abysmal and impersonal pedagogy which sets some children up for miserable lives, even as it serves to further the diabolical aims of globalization.

No, we must remain focused on each child's gifts and spiritual condition, guiding and correcting our course analogous with the spiritual conditions, but always with the *telos*, or end, in mind: purification from the passions and illumination of the *nous*.

This brings us to one final question with regard to worldly wisdom: can one find enlightenment *towards salvation* in the writings of the ancient Greek philosophers or in the men of letters among the heterodox, *in terms of the process of purification of the soul?*

---

80 As St John Chrysostom writes, "It is impossible to treat all…people in one way, any more than it would be right for the doctors to deal with all their patients alike." Περί ιεροσύνης, VI.4 [PG 48]; St John Chrysostom, *Six Books on the Priesthood*, trans. Graham Neville (Crestwood, NY: St Vladimir's Seminary, 1977), p. 142.

It should be clear at this point that for whatever reason we utilize the wisdom of the world in the education of our children, its function is *only preparatory* for the spiritual life. Although a honing of the mind can greatly purify one of wrong thinking, the purification of the passions of the soul has spiritual presuppositions which cannot be fulfilled by even the greatest refinement of the rational intellect, much less the imagination, for purification toward illumination pertains to the *nous* and its cleansing.

Christ the Almighty

St. Gregory Palamas

CHAPTER IV

The Central Place of the Orthodox Academy in the Church's Resistance to Secularism

Lecture for Great Lent
April 1, 2019
St. George Serbian Orthodox Cathedral
Cabramatta NSW Australia

It has been a great joy and a blessing, and I am very grateful to his Grace, Bishop Silouan, for inviting me because I have been immensely enriched by my time with you, with your clergy, with the faithful. I am also grateful to God for many things that I have learned. I hope to God that whatever I have offered, it has been of God and not of myself—that it is God's holy ones that have been speaking because I have nothing—but the Church offers everything for us.

I have come to the conviction, both from my experience but also from everything I have seen over the last eighteen years in Greece, that the Orthodox academy (especially for the youngest children), can be one of the most important bastions and fortresses of the Church going forward. It can be for us an essential element of the refuge of the Church if we are going to survive the violent onslaught of secularism. I do not know if you here in Australia are familiar with the Alamo. Have you heard of the Alamo and the battle back in the nineteenth century? The Alamo was the last stand. I like to say in America "for us, along with homeschooling, the Orthodox academy is our Alamo, it is our last stand against the onslaught of secularism."

We are losing generations of Orthodox Christians because the educational systems in the Western world are not only not helping our children, they are designed to take our children away from us. We must understand this. We must understand the history of compulsory state education for the last 200 years. I gave a lecture on this.[81]

Compulsory state education began at the end of the eighteenth century and beginning of the nineteenth century in Germany and its aim was not for the formation in Christ, or even in the formation *per se* of the children, but the socialization (and in particular, the service) of the next generation towards the formation of a modern state. The aim of this education, in the beginning, had nothing to do with the classical vision of Socrates or of the Trivium (the grammar stage, or the logic stage, or the rhetoric stage), which is the classical educational approach. It had everything to do with creating a modern mechanized state and putting people to work for the sake of that state. So the education was intentionally limited for the masses and they only had higher education for the elite. Over time, throughout the nineteenth century and early twentieth century, especially with the totalitarian regimes of Mussolini, Hitler, and Lenin, you see an explosion of state education precisely for the indoctrination of the people into the socialist, communist, and fascist systems. They saw it as an opportunity, again, to

---

81 See "Have Faith: Examining Homeschooling and Compulsory State Education" earlier in this book.

form and shape the masses. It was not about formation in Christ. Anything but! It was the opposite. The growth of compulsory state education is directly associated with the growth of these anti-Christian regimes, and so not only did that happen for political reasons, but we also have a shift in the vision of what contemporary education is meant to do.

Classically, traditionally, among Christian peoples, we have the ideal, we have the archetype—who is Christ. We have the ideal which is to take someone, and initiate them into virtue, grow them in terms of the virtue, present to them, as St. John Chrysostom says, examples of virtue. That is the main aim of education. It is not knowledge in terms of *gnosis*, in terms of just acquiring academic or technical knowledge. That is not the aim of education. It is the formation in the love of Truth, of acquiring the virtues, of leading a life in Christ in the Church.

At the end of the nineteenth century, especially in America, we now have an inversion, not just a departure but an inversion, because there is no common denominator in multicultural and pluralistic societies. In the nineteenth century, in America, they wanted to enculturate and assimilate masses of immigrants. They wanted an educational system which would serve that purpose. We are very naïve if we think by sending our children to state education, we are not undermining their life in Christ. That is very clear today (I think to everyone) with this long line of departures from the Christian anthropology, in the Christian vision of formation [μόρφωση]. I think it is very obvious to everyone where this is going. It has been going on, not for 10, or 20, or 30, but hundreds of years. It is a vision of man as a fruit directly from the Enlightenment. The Enlightenment of course was the great leap and departure away from the classical vision—the Renaissance was even earlier. So the fruits of the Enlightenment would have been the French Revolution or the Russian Revolution, or the American Revolution. In that context, education was also formed and shaped. John Dewey, a famous educator in the United States, was very influential for the contemporary understanding of what is the center of education. Of course, the center of education today is the child, and egotistically so. Not that the child is going to be formed in Christ, or formed in virtue, or formed in any kind of even ancient Greek or Latin ideal, but that we are going to allow the discovery of the child—we are going to leave him to his devices. It is the inversion of the Christian vision.

One has to understand the immediate need for us to start Orthodox schools. I think what is very encouraging is that without a lot of cooperation we see that happening. It is a matter of salvation for our children. It is a matter of the continuation of the Gospel in the future generations, but also an immediate need. Indeed, we needed it yesterday in terms of protecting our children from delusion and from immorality. Even in countries traditionally Orthodox the need is immense. In Greece, for eighteen years everyone has been saying we need to open up schools run by the Church and not rely on state schools which are undermined and perverted by European liberalism and Marxism. It is hard to make that leap of faith and start a homeschooling co-op, let alone an Orthodox academy. Sometimes you just need to begin, even if you are not entirely ready. With the blessing of our spiritual guides and leaders and with prayer and faith. Such a "start-up" academy was recently[82] blessed to open: the Three Hierarchs Academy in Arizona (where I have been appointed as headmaster).

---

82 In 2018.

Theory

Now, I want to present to you in the next two sections a little about the theory and then about the practice of what I think goes into an Orthodox school.

As I said there are two schools of thought in terms of education. There is the public, Western model that has essentially been developed since the Enlightenment, especially over the last 150 years, which is definitely not an expression of the Christian vision. This is something that we do not want to follow and we reject. Then there is the classical education, which was formed structurally from the time of the ancient Greeks, was consistent throughout all the Roman era, and was picked up in the West too.

So structurally we have some similarities with classical education in the West. The classical education movement, which is very much alive today in America, has had a Renaissance in the last 25 years. There are hundreds of schools that have opened up by Papal and Reformed Protestants in rejection of the public vision, the state schools; they are projecting a classical education. I am going to talk a little about what that is, and what we do not like about it, because again, the Orthodox vision is unique. Some people will say Orthodoxy is like Catholicism without the Pope. Well, this is not classical education with a few things taken away. It is a different vision, but the closest thing to that vision right now, in Western society, is classical education, as it has been understood by many educators today. So, we have to begin there. Again, structurally, it is also akin to what we have done in the past. So if you went back to the thirteenth or fourteenth century, and you wanted to see how St. Gregory Palamas was educated, for instance, or even back to the early fathers, you would see that the basic structure is the same.

First of all, we need to say, that experience is going to all be intimate, as in a family. It was never this mass education that we see today. If you wanted to be highly educated in the fifth to tenth or twelfth century in the Roman Empire, you would have a tutor. You would probably not begin education apart from your mother and father until you were nine or ten years old. The tutor would have come to your house or perhaps you would have gathered together with a few others. There might have been a handful of students around that tutor or maybe a little bit more if there was some particular education for the purpose of serving the Empire. We see in the Roman Empire, there was a desire on the part of the state to have people who were well educated in law, in Latin, and in Greek, to be able to serve the purposes of the state—but these were a very small group of people. Most people who were educated, for the thousand years of the *Romiosini* (the Christian Roman Empire), were educated by the Church. They were not highly educated; they were educated in the basics. The stages they would have passed through, falling along the lines of the ancient Greek education, would have been three stages: grammar, logic or dialectic, and rhetoric. Those are the classic stages as you see in both East and West, and even after the Renaissance in the West.

So what happened? Why do we have a divergence in terms of the vision of education in the East and the West, between the Orthodox and the West? Well, the Renaissance happened. One of the reasons why we have a classical education renaissance in the fourteenth and fifteenth centuries is precisely to get away from classical Christian approaches. So its origins are not necessarily Christian, but they were still seeking to educate them in the basics of grammar, dialectic or logic, and rhetoric. They were learning Latin, and they were learning Greek. This is what it meant to be an educated person in the West—but they were small groups. They are always small groups. It was personal, there was a tutor, and you were learning everything from that tutor. So that is one of the first things we are trying to replicate. We want to keep things small. We want to keep it a family atmosphere. We want to have the children hug their teachers, take the blessing of their priests, and form enduring, lifelong friendships. We want intimate relationships with their teachers. This is how, as I said, education was characterized for most of history: small groups of determined students gathered around their tutor, learning from him not only a narrow corridor of knowledge but lessons for all of life.

The second thing that is key in a traditional, classical, Orthodox education is the partnership with the parents. We also put that forward, first and foremost. We understand that the chief pedagogue—the person who is chiefly responsible for teaching the children—is the parent. We serve the parent, not the other way around. You see, in compulsory education, in state schools, and socialist settings, we have the idea that the state is responsible for the education. So even in Greece today, it is formally illegal to do homeschooling because they consider that as their (i.e., the state's) responsibility. So that is something that is very different in America. In America, surprisingly so in some ways, all 50 states have confirmed that the parents are in charge of the education of the children and not the state. That is why homeschooling in America is flourishing. We have 2.4 million children[83] in America who are homeschooled and there is a treasure of resources available online and in local communities. They are getting together. Many times Orthodox Christians and both Papal and Reformed Protestants are getting together in co-ops. They are working together to educate their children.

---

83 In 2018. In 2021, 3.7 million children were homeschooled.

Today, we see a flourishing of online, classical education sources. So you can go sign your children up, pay a fee, and you have, twice a week through the internet, a personal, live teaching with an educator. It could be ten, fifteen, or twenty kids in that classroom. Online, you see the kids who are there, their names are there, you can raise your hand, you can ask a question, you can see the teacher teach, you can see the blackboard, etc. It is as close as you can imagine to a real classroom. They are meeting twice a week and they are doing things like Latin, Greek, logic, rhetoric, and all the other courses that one would need today in public education. This is happening in the thousands, in terms of courses being offered right now on the internet.

It is important to stress that, if we are going to understand education properly, the parent will give account at the Second Coming for the education of their child. It is very clear in Proverbs that you will give an account. You cannot say, "Well the state took my child, I am not responsible." You are responsible for raising your child *in the fear and the admonition of the Lord*, and a big part of that is going to happen from the time they begin formal education until they go on to university (if they go on to university). So we partner with the parents and it is very important for us that we are there with them, and we are close to them, and they understand that they are a part of the education. Of course, that presupposes that they believe in the education and they want what we are offering (sometimes that is a task in itself). I find myself educating or needing to educate sometimes the parents more than the children in terms of what an Orthodox education is all about.

So this classical, Christian, traditional (call it what you will) Orthodox education, which really is with us from at least the fourth century onward, follows, again, this so-called Trivium: the grammar, logic, and rhetoric stages. We will examine these stages shortly. The grammar stage is from first to fourth grade, roughly. The dialectic or logic stage is from fifth to eighth grade and then ninth to twelfth would be the rhetoric stage. We have that in common with all who strive to do "classical education" today. We could, for example, teach something like Homer, even though the content is somewhat problematic, for language has always been a part of the education of those educated in the Christian Roman Empire (including St. Gregory Palamas). Because of the importance of language, there are certain texts which we are going to employ in an Orthodox Christian setting, with the necessary presuppositions and discernment.

However, in many ways Western classical education diverged from Orthodoxy. It does not express the Orthodox *phronema*, it does not have the common end of our education, which is the acquisition of virtue, that is, the process of purification, illumination, and *theosis* (likeness to Christ) and it does not have the means (how we get there) and the sources. We are looking for the true, the good, and the beautiful. This is a phrase used very often in classical education. The question is unpacking the true, the good, and the beautiful, what it means and how we commune with it. We are going to have a divergence in all three ways to a lesser or greater degree.

In the West there are the so called "great books." The great books were more or less invented and created in the early twentieth century, and it is a list of what you must read if you want to be an educated person. That is how they describe it. In other words, the great books are those increasingly, immensely important texts written by philosophers, literary authors, theologians, historians, and all the rest, that forms the core and the sources for education. The problem is, in the West, those great books, from the Schism on, are going to be books that we are not going to want to have as listed as great books for us. We are not interested in filling our kids with thought which is contrary to Christ, even if it is considered a "great" book. There would be a lot more reticence on the Orthodox part of including, without discernment, all of these texts. Whereas in the West, there is not that kind of discernment present many times, and so those books are included and those ideas are discussed. Sure, we are going to encounter those eventually and even debate them, however, in a more limited scope. We have our own great books, which are ignored in the West. Our writers, have either never been understood or have been forgotten by the West. There is a gap in the West between Augustine and Aquinas for instance. We have St. Maximus the Confessor, St. Symeon the New Theologian, St. Photius the Great, who are not present in the great books of the West. Even after the Schism, totally ignored in the West, you have saints Gregory Palamas, Nikodemos the Hagorite, Seraphim of Sarov and all kinds of other writers. In Greek you can include somebody like Papadiamantis or in Russia, Dostoevsky, although many times you can find Dostoevsky in the West as well. So, the sources differ.

 Also, our ultimate goal and the means of attaining that differ. We are not interested, per se, in what is called the "great conversation," this conversation that has been happening in western society between philosophers, theologians, and scientists. That is not our main interest. In the West, traditionally, the educators want the students to become a part of this great conversation of intellectuals. That is not our goal. We want to have a great conversation, a truly great conversation, but not because we engage every prominent thinker, but rather because we are engaged by exceptionally inspired discourse of heavenly origins. The boast of Orthodox civilization is not the quantity of the works produced (you often hear that in classical circles in the West), nor the rate by which the ideas are exchanged, but rather the quality of the communion generated and the depth of the meaning attained. That is what we are interested in. It is better to have less but go deeper than to have more, have confusion, and have diversion from the one thing needful. So our end, in Orthodoxy, in educational enlightenment, is not merely to produce good wise men and much less good citizens. If this were the case, we would be impoverished as Orthodox, and the incarnation would be rather unnecessary — if that was the goal of our formation. Just as the law was our pedagogue, until faith came, so too, the end of education must be initiation into the Spirit—the beginning of an endless ascent to divine-humanity in the Church.

Our great books could also be explained in the following way: We are not interested in the kind of knowledge that comes from academic research alone, but we want to be initiated into Truth in an experiential way. We want to bring forth people to the knowledge of the truth in a personal and communal way. You can talk about and describe truth in many ways: beauty and goodness, through the study of the great books; but unless one is personally communing with the truth then this beauty, this truth, this goodness that they are discovering in their reading remains in the rational realm and is elusive as an experience. So this part of the Orthodox academy cannot be the study of great books but the encounter with Truth incarnate in the spiritual life, in the people who are teaching the children. The most important element is who is teaching and not what they are teaching, of course — in the experience of the Divine Liturgy and the whole spiritual life of the community. So this truth, beauty and goodness, which is the aim of classical education, is not attained primarily through the rational intellect, but through the *nous*, i.e., the spirit of man. It is clear that the means and the ends toward this are spiritual.

So our educational paradigm is shaped and determined by our Orthodox soteriology (what salvation is about), by our gnosiology (our understanding of knowledge). Our Orthodox understanding of the acquisition of knowledge is not just *gnosis*, which is a kind of intellectual knowledge about something, but as St. Paul says in the Scriptures: *epignosis*, which is experiential knowledge. That is our paradigm in terms of knowledge. If we understand that, then we better understand the role of academic education or the so-called liberal arts in the Orthodox context. It takes on a different role. It is more limited and more particular and it works together with the development of the Spirit and not apart from it. In most places, even in the best classical education, what we are talking about is an academic acquisition of knowledge, and not a spiritual encounter with Truth.

So we will talk quickly about the so-called Trivium, which is the Latin term for this three-fold educational process that people would go through educationally or academically in classical education. We said the first is grammar. It comes from the Greek word *grammatikos* and it means basically the art of using and combining symbols to express thought. This is the building blocks of knowledge. This is why the grammar stage is the first four years. At this age, children are well-disposed to learning about numbers (also acquiring with them), facts, and dates (such as found in their history lessons). This is the time period that we need to give them the raw material of education. We are not going to engage them in terms of the rational argumentation, the logic stage. We are not going to expect from them rhetoric, expressing of ideas. That is not what is going to happen in the first four years. We are going to give them the basics, the building blocks. They are going to be filled with that and then when they reach maturity, the next stage. They are going to pass from that into the art of thinking, and that is the dialectic stage, the logic stage. Here they learn the mechanics of thought and analysis, the art of formal and material reasoning. That is the dialectic stage. We are in the sixth through eighth, or ninth grades. Then the rhetoric stage is the final stage in the Trivium. So that is when we are getting into the high school. Now, they have got the building blocks. They have honed their rational understanding, their logic, their dialectic. It is time to express and to apply the knowledge they have acquired in order to instruct and to persuade. This is very important in classical education.

St. Gregory Palamas, if you remember from his life, when he was eighteen and just before he left for the monastery, he presented in front of the Emperor and chief officer and preeminent scholar Theodore Metochites. They were surprised by the analysis of Aristotle by St. Gregory and Metochites told the Emperor, "Even Aristotle himself, if he were present and had heard this young man, would in my opinion praise him more than a little [beyond measure]... those who study philosophical treatises, especially the complex works of Aristotle, should possess such a spirit and aptitude."[84] So the rhetoric was the sign that somebody was educated—he could express himself, persuade others, and the knowledge or understanding was then transmitted as wisdom. This meant the person had arrived at wisdom. We could put it more simply: grammar pertains to the thing as it is symbolized, dialectic pertains to the thing as it is known, and rhetoric pertains to the thing as it is communicated. So

---

84 Philotheos Kokkinos, *Gregory Palamas: The Hesychast Controversy and the Debate with Islam, Documents relating to Gregory Palamas*, translated by Norman Russell (Liverpool: Liverpool University Press, 2022), pp. 61-62.

it is symbols, knowledge, and communication. This is the process by which one becomes an educated human being.

If we were to stop there, we would pretty much have described classical education as it is lived out and understood among the non-Orthodox, but now, much more, we have to actually give the heart. We have talked about the head and the rational intellect and its development, which is essential; but where is the heart? Where is the spirit? Here we have the three-fold, let us say spiritual trivium, or three-fold program of purification, illumination, and deification. If we did not have that, the (academic) trivium is vanity. It is not salvific. It could actually puff one up and lead him into delusion. This is the danger with academic, intellectual, and rational knowledge, that if not combined with spiritual ascent—with purification from the passions, with humility and all the virtues—it is working against our salvation. So it is key, that at the core of our Orthodox academy, we have the spiritual trivium or spiritual three-fold process of formation. Toward achieving the overall formation of the child (and precisely because there should be no compartmentalization, and thus secularization of the children's lives), the academy has to have, as a central role, the overall furtherance of the children's spiritual ascent.

So if you are forming or building an academy, and the parents want to send their kids to this academy, everyone has to be on the same page here. If they are expecting their kids to go just to a better school, a school that does things in a nice, Orthodox context, but they are not expecting spiritual formation, then what are we doing? We have not done an Orthodox school. We are not on the path of Orthodox education. The core has to be the therapy, the restoration of the spiritual, of the spirit of man, the *nous* of man. If the academic trivium is meant to bring the rational intellect to a knowledge of creation, the spiritual trivium is essential for the spirit of man, the *nous*, to come to an experiential knowledge of God. Whereas the formal schooling process of learning is necessarily limited. The process of returning to God and increasing the depth of communion with Him has a beginning but it has no end. Therefore, the school is just the beginning of this whole process. So when the ultimate aim, the ultimate goal of salvation in Christ is purposefully sought in the spiritual process of purification, illumination, and glorification, then the academic trivium comes as a firm support and itself finds its fulfillment. So these two have to go together, it is like body and soul. Otherwise you do not have an Orthodox academy.

What is the aim of a traditional Orthodox education, simply put? Within the Orthodox fullness, and the freedom of Christ, a critical and creative thinker is in a position to decipher the *zeitgeist*, the spirit of the age. So we are teaching people not just what they need to know; we are not just preparing them to be a part of a system to get a job. We are teaching them how to learn, and continually learn throughout their whole life. Learning how to learn. We seek to free them so that they can be themselves, free of the shackles of this age. To throw off the shackles, to make the faith and truth of the Church his own, to live for Christ, with his whole heart, mind, and soul. That is the goal of an Orthodox education.

It is the exact opposite, in my experience and understanding, with state compulsory education. It is not to free them, but to enslave them, and to make them a part of the system, which, ultimately, will serve the Antichrist. So we have to be very clear, the goal of our academy, and that is freedom from the shackles of the age, not simply preparation to serve the society which is being formed.

Practice

Enough on the theory of the curriculum and education. Let us talk about some practical aspects then we can open it up for questions. I am going to give you what I think, and I am going to take largely from an important Orthodox academic educator today, his name is David Hicks. He has written a book called *Norms and Nobility*. I highly recommend it. Anybody who is going to be your academic dean or chair needs to read it at their school. *Norms and Nobility*. He was an educator in the classical Western context for decades. He was in Athens, and now he is back in America. He became an Orthodox Christian, I am not sure when, maybe about a decade ago, and he has been writing and talking to Orthodox people about an Orthodox education. And so largely I am going to take from him because I like it and I think it is expressive of the Orthodox *phronema* on this question. He gives seven traits of an Orthodox education, seven traits of an Orthodox academy. Here is the first (and I am going to comment as we go, adding a few of my own thoughts).

The first and most important thing, of course, are the relationships that are built into the academy—that means the teacher. The teacher is the most important. If you have a school that has teachers who are not living the spiritual life, do not have an Orthodox *phronema*, do not understand what the end of Orthodox education is, then you do not have an Orthodox school. The school is as good as its teachers. So first and foremost, we have to have a faithful and spiritually mature Orthodox group of teachers and they need to demonstrate their love in actions for the children. That is number one.

Number two is that we need to develop Orthodox Christian community. It is one of the biggest missing pieces of the puzzle in our Orthodox life today. Because we live in a society which is individualistic, which is compartmentalized, which is disintegrating the community. The whole structure of the Western community (especially America and Australia, and other places) is that it does not have roots, does not have an identity, and we are all individuals, and so the community is being lost. We have to create them. The Orthodox school is a tremendous opportunity for the Church to increase the community, to bind together the children from a young age, in their Orthodox identity. They must cease to exist as individuals, and their relationship with God and one another has to come alive, and that is really important. It needs to be a conscious goal of the academy to create community. So number two would have to be Orthodox community.

There is a wonderful, wonderful historical example that Dr. Hicks mentions. Let me just share that with you. I did not know about this until I read his writings. In the fourth century, there was a school in Nisibis. It was re-established by St. Ephraim the Syrian in Edessa, after the city fell to the Persians. The supreme authority in the school was exercised in community meetings where the students, because of their numbers, had the deciding vote and elected the educators, or the head of the educators. In other words, the people handled all the finances and operations of the school, along with the discipline. So the head of the school was the director, the spiritual guide and the director of studies. No one could be expelled from the school without a vote of the community. If you just consider that a minute, this means they had a high degree of trust between teachers and students. This was something that I think we definitely should imitate. The students need to be a part, and feel that they own the school. They need to be a part of the school. It should not be something that they just come to and leave. They need to help clean up, they need to help raise money for the school, they need to be a part of the whole process. That is a great example from Church history, which I did not know about.

Number three: It is key that we have the right criteria for choosing the content or the sources that the children are going to be reading. One of the keys here is that they have a vertical component. Whatever they are going to read, it cannot always be Orthodox material. It cannot be, because there is not enough Orthodox material in the English language to provide for our needs. So we are going to be using non-Orthodox sources whether we like it or not. So, on what basis do we choose what we are going to use? Well, there has to be a vertical dimension. There has to be God as part of the story or we should not include it at all. Much of the material that is being used in contemporary education is godless. It is only horizontal. It is not vertical. So that has to be the basic prerequisite.

So, there are sources out there that we can use. We need to go back in our academy, we need to do historical research. We should go back to the nineteenth century texts, even in some cases to math texts from the mid-1800s. Go back to McGuffey readers, for example, which was a nineteenth century series of educational and English-language texts, to see what they were doing then. We believe that after this renovation in education, especially the end of the nineteenth century, we had a perversion, distortion, and an undermining of education.

So phonics, for instance, went out the window. People became more and more illiterate. They knew how to read and yet they did not read, and they do not read today. There are many illiterate people in the twentieth century which is very strange and odd—you have people who cannot read. Phonics was the system in place, the way of learning how to read for young children. We are using phonics, that is just one example. You can go back and you can see how they did mathematics. So we are going to go back to the tried and traditional and old ways of educating.

In addition to this, a text should not, of course, celebrate sin in any way. It should put forth the virtues. That would be other criteria for what kind of texts we should incorporate in the educational process. We need to largely throw out the textbooks. Maybe not for mathematics or science but definitely for English, and largely for history. Throw out textbooks, get to the sources. Have the children come into contact directly with sources, with the literature of the day and with the historical sources used to write the history books. If you are teaching the children with textbooks you have an intermediary between the child and the history or the source that you are introducing. You have, in other words, a gatekeeper who is going to keep them from a direct encounter and that is a totally different education. So for instance, if you are reading about the Middle Ages, read about the Middle Ages. Read sources from the Middle Ages. We have that at our disposal. We do not need to have a twentieth century academic who is writing about the Middle Ages to teach us about the Middle Ages. We should go right to the sources. At the very least, if there is a need for a textbook, there are plenty of good, traditional, Christian sources that we can choose that are better than what they are using in the public schools. So we have to bravely tread the path that is not taken by the majority.

Number four: We need to be sure and know that there is no academic disadvantage to our students in failing to study the cultural sources that are filling our society today. We do not need to follow the Jones' and read what they are reading. There is not going to be any academic problem if we do that. We can find our own sources, our own way of imparting culture and knowledge. It is not only because the works we study in Orthodox schools are more demanding, more full of meaning, richer and closer to the source, but because the most researched and data supported educational theory decrees it so.

In other words, what you teach is not nearly as important as how you teach it. This is Dr. Hicks' conclusion and I wholeheartedly agree. We focus a lot on the "what"; we do not understand that "how" you teach and "who" is teaching is far more important than "what" you are teaching. The whole classical education approach, the whole traditional Christian approach could be summed up as: we are interested in teaching them how to fish and not just giving them a fish to eat. This is a very different approach than what is going on in most education today. Dr. Hicks says the following, which I like to quote (it is very, very good in terms of rational thinking, critical thinking, problem solving, which of course is an aim of the school). He says, "We ought to have clear instructional protocols that ask all teachers to use an interrogatory method based on high order reasoning," and goes on to explain himself. "A teacher needs to identify the essential questions for every lesson." So you go into a lesson and you know what to ask. That is a part of the Socratic method if you are going to get them to think deeply, and to have critical thought, and not just be passive receptors regurgitating what the teacher said. We do not want that.

Yet, most of education today is educating for the test. Most of the education is preparing somebody to take a test. This is a terrible way of educating. It undermines true love of knowledge and it creates people who are indifferent to truth. We want them to have critical thinking, and questions are the key. The educator has to ask the right questions. Many times, we do not want to just give them food. "Here it is. Here is the truth." No. They need to be troubled. They need to be challenged. They need to be provoked to think about, understand, and come to the knowledge of the truth on their own, expending a lot of energy to do that. A teacher needs to do this. He or she needs to use differentiated strategies and instruction, a variety of strategies, not just one dimensional (not just lectures, not just discussion), but a variety of things to keep education lively. Never complete a lesson without a high order assessment. In other words, at the end you have to bring it back and summarize and present the conclusion so we have closure and a clear understanding. Without this, the teacher will not build the critical thinking, complex problem solving, high order reasoning skills that the people need today, if they are going to be free of the *zeitgeist*, if they are going to be also very successful in terms of their future. They will not be faithful to the best traditions of Orthodox Christians. He says, "Remember we are nurturing humans not automatons, creatures whom their Creator made in His own image with reasoning minds and free wills. The conclusions that our students come to after having weighed all the evidence and heard all the arguments, are those that will guide them against the intellectual fads and fancies of the world. At the same time, it is providing them with critical tools to tackle any new topic or question with confidence and discernment."

Number five: Dr. Hicks says we have a theology of history. We have a narrative that culminates in the incarnation. It starts with the incarnation and culminates in the incarnation, passion, resurrection, the Second Coming, all of these events in time that made everything new. We are not just wandering through history. We have the Alpha and the Omega. We understand where we are coming from, where we are going. I would say at the center then of everything, has to be that we organize the school along the Church calendar, its feasts and its fasts, its saints' days, its readings from the Gospel, epistles and Lives of the Saints. This is a part of our school curriculum and our school life. It ought to some extent reflect the prayers of the church, the books we study: to draw on the themes of our Orthodox narrative and God's redemptive work in history. This should call attention to the shallowness and the emptiness and the depravity of the world absent God, the godless world that we live in, contrasted with the hope and redemption in Christ. It needs to have both. You cannot just talk about Christ and have a positive assessment. You do need a critique. You do need critical thinking. You do need, at times, even mockery of the absurdity of much of what is passing as civilized society today. The children need to have that protection; they need to have that critical thinking.

In this vein, I taught the *Orthodox Survival Course* by Father Seraphim Rose, which I highly recommend you all read, as it is an assessment of the whole process of the apostasy. How we have arrived, why we have arrived, and what we have in the Western world. It goes back all the way to the Schism. He explains step by step the process of the dissolution of the Christian vision in the West. It is all connected. It is not *at all* isolated. What we are living in the twenty-first century is connected all the way back to the eleventh century. Father Seraphim lays it out. It is his *Orthodox Survival Course*. These were lectures he gave to young men in the 1970s and it was a fruit of all his research that he had done, before and after becoming an Orthodox Christian. That is the kind of thing that we should bring to the Orthodox school. That kind of critical thinking, that kind of Orthodox *phronema* and worldview, which assesses everything and gives us the Alpha and the Omega. If we do not have that, then we are lost in history. We will not understand what is happening to us. We will not understand the society we live in. Then if our children go out there, without that understanding, they are going to be victims of this, of this *zeitgeist*, of this spirit of the age that we are living through.

Dr. Hicks teaches that we should be very clear that the state school's narrative is much more shocking, much more anti-historical than ours. Because many times people say, "Well if that's what you are doing in there, this is not education, this is indoctrination." This is one of the things you might hear from somebody who talks about an Orthodox school. "You are indoctrinating people! You are not allowing them to be free." In fact, it is just the opposite. They are getting indoctrination in the state schools. We are not indoctrinating more than the state's schools, wherein religion is a proscribed topic. You do not talk about God in the state schools. He is never mentioned. Of course there, God as the God of history is not a part of the educational process. So we are far freer and we actually free people from the chains. So we should not have any kind of complex when people accuse us of teaching doctrine and teaching a vision of the world, as if they are not doing the same thing in the state schools. They are doing it, and they are bringing people into nihilism and hopelessness because [for them] there is no God. There is no point to life without God.

The sixth point is here, and then we will quickly end with the seventh. He says here, that the ancient Greeks, who invented the school (as you probably all know, the ancient Greeks invented the academy), did not distinguish in their language between education and culture. When seeing the word *paideia* in Greek, modern English translators have to decide from the context whether to write education or culture. It is interchangeable in Greek. That is very instructive for us. It is an important lesson. Culture is the most profound education of all. So our schools have to be about producing Orthodox culture, the Orthodox ethos, the Orthodox way of life. If all we do is give them education, and even Orthodox education, we have failed. When they go to school, they want to, they have to, go and feel they are entering into a whole culture, a whole way of living and understanding, and it has to pervade everything.

Culture is perpetually indoctrinating and educating us whether we are aware of it or not. Think of the profound effects that television and video games and social media have on our children. This is the kind of culture we are living in. All of that is forming (deforming) our children. The television, and everything that is going on in modern media, is educating; and it is culture. So the same thing has to happen in the Orthodox context if we are going to have any success. If we fail in that, then we are going to fail the children, because it is not going to be enough to resist the temptations of the world. The temple, of course, is the center of that. The worship, of course, is the center of this culture. It has to be the Divine Liturgy. The worship has to be the center. So there are unique traditions in the Orthodox Church which shape our taste, our habits, and our attitudes, and that should be a part of the mission of the Orthodox academy.

Finally, Dr. Hicks suggests (and I think this is something that would be very practical as well as an important pedagogical end) when education ends, when they are ending their time in the Orthodox academy, before they go on to other things, it should all be summarized. This should be a culminating course of reflection upon all that they have learned, and the Orthodox priest or bishop or monk should be at the center of that culminating process. He should be there to guide them and make sense of and unify everything they have learned. Included in that should be contact with the monastery and an essay explaining everything they have learned. They need to summarize and look at it all as a united whole, and not as a bunch of knowledge, and not as a bunch of experiences. Rather, they need to make sense of that at the end. This will be something that will be with them the rest of their lives.

So I hope I have given you a sense of the struggle of what it means to open up an academy, how important it is for our Church today everywhere to care for our children in the realm of education, what an academic curriculum would be like, the principles upon which it would be based, and then some practical, important aspects of what an Orthodox academy contains. This could be food for thought, and hopefully for lots of good questions. Thank you very much for your attention.

Hieromonk Seraphim (Rose)

Q&A SESSION

from "The Central Place of the Orthodox Academy in the Church's Resistance to Secularism"

QUESTION 1:

Concerning "teaching to the exam" and the SAT.

In the United States, we have the SAT (or ACT, there are different tests). I think pretty much every country has something like this. Mainly (but not only) on the basis of that, in the United States, you will try to enter the university of your choice. Education, in America and I guess it is the same in Australia, is really gauged toward that exam. They are preparing you for that and want you to get good scores because it is going to come back to them in state money and all kinds of things. So the question is, as an Orthodox Christian, how does an Orthodox school approach this and the success of students based on these exams? An Orthodox Christian school should not (I repeat, "not") teach to the exam.

The fact of the matter is, in public education, it is all dumbed down. The standards are lower than a classical, Orthodox education. The things they are doing to prepare you are much less than if you would just focus on a classical, Christian, traditional education. If you do that, you will do fine on the exam. I have a lot of examples, personally, which prove that. In a classical education, from a young age, you are learning Greek and Latin. If you have two, three, four, five years of Greek and Latin, learn it well, then you are going to fly on the English part of that exam. It is going to be easy. If you learn Latin, for instance, you learn all the etymology, the words and how they are made up, then you go deeper into the meaning of the story or whatever you are reading. So it gives you much more than this dumbed down state education. State education has to be dumbed down, it has to be the lower common denominator, because they are not interested in working with those two, or three, or five students (out of the thirty) and running with them and bringing them higher and higher. They have to keep everyone at the level of the medium, if not lower. So there is no reason to have any anxiety on the part of the Orthodox school with "how are we going to prepare them for the exam?" They are going to do better on the exam without any need to follow the standards of the state, because the standards of the state are lower and intentionally so. If you are following this classical education, you are learning Trivium, the languages, you are learning to express yourself in rhetoric, and think logically, and all the rest, then you are going to do fine on the exam.

I have personal examples of this. My son did extremely well and never went through any public education and did not prepare for the SAT in any particular way. So this is a good question, because that is one of the big questions my parents had. "How am I going to get into college? How am I going to do the SAT?" There is unreasonable anxiety about that. We do not have that knowledge, so we think there is that need to do what they do in the state schools.

QUESTION 2:

Concerning how texts are to be read and analyzed.

So you have a text, a source, or the Bible, or some kind of patristic teaching, or any kind of philosophical text, or any kind of literary text. The student is going to come in contact with that. He is going to read it on his own. Depending on the age group, the role of the teacher is going to be discussion. With the older age groups there really will not be much lecturing at all. The discussion will be guided discussion, using the Socratic Method so that the students are exploring with a guide. Now obviously, the guide is the teacher: the first and most important person. The guide, as I said earlier, has to be a spiritually mature, faithful, and educated Orthodox Christian. Otherwise, the school is not going to have success. The presupposition is the teacher does not only have an experience (which will guide them in interpretation) but that he will be resting on the guidance and interpretation of the Saints, the Church, and the collective wisdom of the Church. So the two things that will guide them: the personal experience and the patristic witness. So it is not going to be a free-for-all. It is not going to be my opinion.

Sometimes, people do Bible studies (even sometimes Orthodox) and it is "Tell me how you feel when you read that text." That is not the Orthodox approach. No one cares about our own feelings and our own perspectives in that sense. We are looking to enter into the meaning of the author and what he is trying to communicate to us. We are looking at that in the context of the Truth, which is incarnate, and the truth which is taught in the Church. So in that context, I do not see any kind of major intermediary who is going to mislead us into danger. Now if you do not have those presuppositions, if you do not have that context, then of course there are going to be problems.

Again, it is the most important decision you are going to make as a school and as a dean of the school, that is, who are your teachers. I would say, in my experience, that is something you should spend a lot of time on, think deeply about, and do a lot of work to find the best teachers, before you open up the school. Of course, the dean is going to be the most important decision of all. The vision must be laid out here. It is a difficult time for us. As I said, we are path-finders. There is nothing which exists as a whole, ready-made, and ready to go. We are collecting all the wisdom that we see but we are still having to form that and put it into practice. It is a process until we arrive at a point where we have surety and clarity, and we can initiate the children into that wisdom we want to give them in the texts.

QUESTION 3:

Concerning continuing education then and now.

After the Trivium, there is the Quadrivium, which would be the sciences in the ancient world, which are different than our contemporary sciences. The Quadrivium would have been arithmetic, geometry, music, and astronomy. Then after that, there would have been a select few that went onto Philosophy. Philosophy would have been the final stage of an education for somebody, even up to the fall of the Empire in the 15th century. In the 19th and 20th centuries, there is a very developed system of PhDs and post-PhDs and you do not see that [in the ancient world]. There is not the breadth of subject matter; they did not have the things we have today in terms of what to learn. So you have to adapt this [traditional approach] to contemporary society. You cannot just stick with what they did 500 years ago. There are other things to learn. The goal is not to give them knowledge, quantitatively. The goal is to initiate them into the wisdom and the understanding so they continue to learn throughout their life. We are not going to be obsessed with filling their brains with material. That is not a true education; it does not rest on that. So they [the traditional educators] were pretty narrow. At the top of the pyramid, was philosophy. In other words, the whole quest of wisdom and understanding. In the Orthodox context, it would be including theology and the Orthodox teachings of the Fathers.

QUESTION 4:

Concerning the world forcing its needs upon the school's development.

The problem you [the questioner] are presenting is not unlike the problem already presented in society in terms of a workplace or a job when they are requiring similar views to be accepted in this context. I think that there is this practical way of getting through the hoops and making it happen. I am sure there is a way that the school can stay true to its vision and yet (if they know they have to deal with particularly this text and that text and another text), they have special sessions with students who are going to prepare for the test and get them through it. God forbid, practically helping kids through the hoops becomes a part of the true education of the school. This is one option.

I think, though, we are exponentially jumping ahead, i.e., time is passing exponentially faster. Things are not like 100 years ago, because of technology, because of political systems, and all the rest. I do not think it is too far in the future when even this option is problematic. We have to prepare ourselves, whether it is in the school setting or whether it is in the society to say "What are the boundaries?" and "We do not need that." I know asking such questions is not going to be popular (you are starting a school and want to get them into college). But, I guarantee you (humanly speaking if I can do that) this will be a real question five or ten years down the road. Eventually, at some point, it will be a question we ask. "Are we a part of this or are we not a part of this?" For the time being, we can get through the hoops, I hope. However, it is only a matter of time until we are faced with hard choices, because they are going to ask us to regurgitate lies about man and God to be able to pass those tests. What are we going to do? It reminds me of the Christians' reaction to the Pharisees: Are we going to be put out of the synagogue? Are we going to accept that? Are we going to go with the Lord outside the gate? That is the kind of decision that is going to be coming down the road.

We are trying to introduce sacred chant. I want to add iconography and other sacred art. We are going to develop an athletics aspect, but of course it is very basic now since we do not have the facilities. That is all a part of our education. I should have added this to my talk, next semester, we want to have (after school) home economics. Back in the day, they taught you how to sew, how to be a homemaker, how to fix cars, how to plant a garden, woodworking, etc. All the practical stuff that is not being taught today is making us useless; we are academic intellectuals who cannot use their hands. So that has got to be a part of our education as well. Initially it will be an after-school option for the kids and for the community. That is our goal for next semester. All of that going forward is going to be part of our education, not just the rational academics, but also the practical things kids need very much to learn.

QUESTION 5:

Concerning how the parents and adults in the school effectively work towards its future.

I think there is great need for schools for parents—schools to teach them to parent. We do not necessarily learn that. Who learns to be a parent until they start being a parent? It would be very helpful if there were particular classes offered to help them understand what it means to be an Orthodox Christian parent today. Secondly, they need to be very much a part of the school. They need to own it. It needs to be a communal thing. They need to come and volunteer and work at the school. They need to help promote the school and all the rest of it. There has to be this, otherwise it will not be successful. Thirdly (the question of the future and what is happening sociologically), I read a survey, and believe it to be true, of Greek descendants in America. What percentage of the descendants of Greek immigrants remained Orthodox? It was a startling conclusion; eighty percent of Greek descendants had left the Church. They are totally indifferent, or became Protestants, or became something else other than Orthodox. The question is: Why? Why did so many people in the Greek Archdiocese leave the Church? Let us say it is fifty percent. It is still an amazing number. I think a good part of the reason is the refusal of the Church to deal with the reality that you have to put roots down where you are and provide shade, spiritually, for them in the place that they are living. Whether you like it or not, the second and third and fourth generation is going to call that place home. They are going to look at that, increasingly, as their identity. That is the fruit of immigration. That is very clear in the book of Ruth and other places. Pastorally, we can close our mind to that and say "let's double down on our ethnic identity." Some people will embrace that. Many will not. The percentages in America show it. So you have got to figure out a way to feed immediately those in the culture and language of the people and at the same time, start to develop a program for the day after, for the next stage, for the children and for the children's children; that they will own it and identify with it.

That means mission. That means outreach. That means that the Church is, by its nature, making disciples—not just preaching, not just teaching, making disciples (which is very different, disciples means initiation into the mystery, it means someone who is obedient and submits to the Church, it requires the mind of Christ). There is no easy solution. We are spiritually attacked on all sides. We have got a demonic onslaught through what is going on in the society surrounding us. Nonetheless, we have the truth and when you preach the truth prophetically, people find peace. That is what I have learned: when the prophetic voice of Christ is communicated, people embrace it and they find meaning.

What is all of this going on around us? It is nihilism. It is meaninglessness. That is what is going on around us. They do not know where they are going. They do not know whence they have come. They have lost the Alpha and the Omega. They are at sea in philosophies, theories, and demonic activities. We have the upper hand in many ways. However, because we are silent or because we are afraid to speak the truth to our own people (saying, "look, this is what we got to do, and you have to deal with it…"), we do not want to go there. It is comfortable. We are comfortable. But it is not going to last forever.

Now, getting back to the school for a minute. I wanted to say it and neglected to say it earlier: At the heart of the education in the Orthodox context (and it is a change from this Trivium) is the Lives of the Saints. We are going to be doing the following in our education. The first four years, we are not going to talk about history much; we are not going to talk about science much; we are not going to go into other cultures and traditions. We are going to look and focus on examples of virtue for the children. That is going to be the basis of the whole education. Everything else they are going to be taught later on, when they meet other cultures, other traditions, other peoples, it is going to be filtered through the vision of Christ, in history, the continuation of the Incarnation in the Lives of the Saints. That is going to be their criteria. The first four years are the most important years in terms of education. That foundation needs to be laid during that time. Without that, I think, the whole rest of their education is going to be in danger of being lopsided and rationalistic. The spirit of God, the leaven, is not going to be there.

So that is why every morning after prayer, in our school, all the kids gather in the main area (52 kids) and I begin to teach them the life of the saint for that day. I do not just do it by opening the book and reading it to them. I have a large screen behind me. I use Google Maps and say, "Let us go from Arizona and fly to..." wherever the saint lived. "Here is where the saint lived." We look at our timeline. I say, "Here is our timeline." I talk to them again, and again, about our timeline. I want them to get a sense of the whole history of the Church. I say, "Where is the fourth century? Show me the fourth century. Here is where this saint lived in the fourth century." I talk about the fourth century. They get the context, the time and space in which the saint lived. Like Christ, He came in time and space and lived like us. Implicitly I am teaching them "You can be like Him. This is not just for the monks on Athos. This is for everyone." Then we begin. We look at the icon of the saint. They see it is a human being just like them. Then we begin to go through the life of the saint. We focus on the virtues of the saint. We say, "This is what the saint did. . . . This is how the saint lived. . . ." Then I recap and I say, "Now you tell me what virtues did you see in the life of the saint? How can we imitate the virtues of the saint so we can become like them?" That is how we begin every day in our school. That is the foundation.

I think this has to be happening in our lives, not just in our schools. It is how we should begin our day and our life. We should have the Synaxarion and Lives of the Saints continually open before us. Otherwise, all these other bad examples are going to delude, confuse us, and drag us down. We have to shut those out. Turn off the television. Turn off all the garbage. Focus on the Lives of the Saints and imitating them. I think, God willing, if we stay afloat for three years (the first three years are the hardest time), they say the school will continue for a long time. If we can stay afloat, if these kids stick around (especially the young kids), if they stay with us for ten years, and they hear again and again and again the Lives of the Saints, they are going to be prepared to meet any kind of challenge, spiritually speaking. So that is a big part that I am sorry I neglected it because I think it is huge in an Orthodox context.

QUESTION 6:

Concerning how the school handles its existence in a foreign community and its struggle against urbanization.

The whole question of community and urbanization, yes. Well, I am very happy this school has 176 acres and it is out, somewhat, in the country, not too far. I think we are in a similar situation. We are out in the country. We are far away from the urbanization.

The question is: How do we deal with urbanization? How do I deal with a loss of community? Urbanization is a huge reason why we have secularism in the Church today. If you go back to the 1950s and 60s, that is when, in Greece, the exodus from the villages began. First they left to Thessaloniki and Athens, then they left for Australia and America. I am sure the same happened in Serbia. It is the same process everywhere. The villages emptied. What happened to that villager? The simple, good, God-loving man or woman left, and is now in a city of two million or one million, and the churches are now twenty minutes down the road, and there are probably 150 or 200 people that he never sees except in church on Sunday, if he even gets to know that person. We are talking about a sea change in terms of community and in terms of the spiritual life.

So in the village, they had a common center and that was the church. The church was the social center as much as the spiritual center. They were there every Sunday. In fact, in the village up in Greece, where I was for ten years, the old-timers would tell me when they were kids, the school was right next to the church and they were prepared, by the teacher on Saturday (because they had school on Saturday along with Monday through Friday), for the boys, one by one, to read the epistle in church. Then they went in church, all lined up in their school uniforms (all together, very studiously). It was a part of their life as villagers and students. Their life was one organic seamless garment.

Now they have gone to the urban setting and all of that is lost. Life becomes impersonal. Let us put it in the very basic moral level; there is no one there to call them to accountability. "Where were you on Sunday, friend? Why were you not in church?" They are not hearing the positive peer-pressure they had from the village setting. So this has had the number one effect and it is the number one problem. It brought about secularism more than any other historical change in modern Greece. More than all the –isms (humanism, ecumenism, phyletism) that is what helps give birth to secularism because the church is no longer incarnate, it loses that community. You do not see that we are all part of the Body of Christ.

So how do we solve it? There is no easy solution, but what people are trying to do (and in Arizona this is certainly what has happened and it is not something that has been organized by one person, it is a movement of God's Holy Spirit) is leave the urbanized centers and different parts of the United States and they are coming and living next to the monastery and they are intentionally living in community. So there is not an easy solution. You have to, now, intentionally create community if you want to have community. The problem is, many times, that there are attempts that fail. Why? Why is there failure in this? Because, it becomes (what many people call) a "hot house." It is not sober. It is not humble. There is a lot of immaturity and zeal not according to knowledge. It is a very delicate thing to create community. It has to be done by people who are prepared to be patient. When you were in the village with 200, or 500, or 700 other people, you did not choose who they were. You did not choose your cousins and aunts and uncles and all the brothers and sisters. That is who you were and you had no choice that was your village. You lived there, whether you liked it or not. However, when you do an intentional community, if you do not really like the person down the street, you can get up and leave. Oftentimes, that is what happens. To create that community which then enables us and supports us in the spiritual life, returns us to normalcy in terms of communal life. What we live on a daily basis is abnormal, it is not human. It is not human to live in small little apartments in large buildings and see no one most of the week, and to work fifty hours, and all the stuff that goes into urbanization. This is not normal and not human. It is inhuman and anti-evangelical and it makes it hard to live the life of the Gospel.

So yes, intentional living, but with a lot of patience, humility, meekness, and obedience. Otherwise it is not going to be successful. You can come together, but you are not going to stick together. You are not going to be together because we are not prepared to do what it takes to stay together. It has to be intentional. Anyone who goes to a monastery will know that to stay there is a crucifixion. It is not "how wonderful!" and "how easy!" It is a crucifixion. That is, of course, salvific. That is who we are. The cross is who we are and that is salvation for us. Nonetheless, you have to be prepared to do what it takes to live in that.

So the school is a wonderful development, if people can start to see it as the center around which the children will gather, around which the Church will gather. I understand that a bishop's quarters is being built there and he will be there as well, which is tremendous. You can see that as a potential center for the Serbian Orthodox and the larger Orthodox community.

Let me also say this (because I wanted to say it earlier but I forgot). There is going to be a great danger of two extremes that the school needs to avoid. One is this idea that we are going to make the school into our Serbian Orthodox Enclave. We are going to make it into something like (negatively speaking) a ghetto. We are going to go there. We are going to close the doors around us. We are going to protect ourselves from anything that is going to threaten our Serbian Orthodox identity. That will be a major failure if that happens. That will not last. It is the same kind of hot-house and lack of sobriety, maturity, and humility that is not based on the Gospel. It is based on our worldly identity as Serbians. It is not going to last because if it is not divine-human, if it is not inspired by the Spirit of God, if it is not Christ at the center of it all, it does not bring fruits. So we have got to be careful. Yes, that is going to be the place where the traditions and the identity are going to be celebrated and going to flourish. Not in a way that is just human, it has got to be divine-human. Christ at the center. If Christ is the center, even those who do not have the Serbian identity will embrace it and rejoice in it. They will not be threatened by the Serbian / Serbian Orthodox title in the school. I think it is a key thing going in to consciously keep that in mind, because there is that temptation on the right, which does not seem to really be a temptation. It actually seems to be really good; "let us focus on that." No! It is going to be there, if Christ is there. You do not need to focus on it. Just like people in Greece, they do not need to focus on being Greek. They just are Greek. When you go to America and you meet Greek-Americans, they have to put that Greek identity out there because they are threatened by the non-Greek community. This is strange for a Greek person in Greece, sometimes, to encounter a Greek-American. "What is wrong with you?" It is like some kind of complex. We do not need that. Just be who you are and if that is in Christ, it is glorious and it attracts people. Forgive me for taking the boldness to say that but I wanted to say that because it is important for us to understand that dynamic. We are not in Serbia so it is not going to be the same kind of environment and experience that would be in Serbia; it is outside of that homogeneous society. So you have got to deal with that pastorally and spiritually if it is going to be successful. That goes for the school as much as the large community that will gather around it.

The other extreme would be to secularize it [the school] and make it into a place where we are going to water it down. One of the big temptations of any school is the following: We get to a critical mass and economically, we cannot make it. We cannot keep it going because we do not have the funds or we do not have the means. So the students start to dwindle. Inevitably, the question is: should we open it up? Should we make it acceptable to anyone and anything? Should we put water in our wine to keep the thing going? I have told my co-workers: "It is better we close than we lose our Orthodox identity." You see it again and again. Harvard University started as a theological school for Protestants; today, of course, it has nothing to do with Protestantism, even Protestant theology, in terms of being true to their roots, I mean. There are untold examples of that in the history of the United States. A religious community starts very devoted to a particular identity but over time that all is lost because they are interested more in keeping the doors open or success economically, then they start to lose their identity. So I think that would be the other extreme, to keep the thing going we start to change our identity to fit in and all the rest. Today and tomorrow, I do not think this is a threat. But in twenty years, in thirty years, it may be. Again, that will not be avoided if Christ is not at the center.

It has to be Christ-centered criteria. The people are going to come for Christ whether they are Serbian or not. Then it is going to be about the Gospel. Then those two extremes are avoided. If that is not there, then we can fall into one of those two extremes.

QUESTION 7:

Concerning the relationship of the school with parishes.

The parish is the community, but the school is a Pan-Serbian community where people from different parishes would meet. I am not saying the school should supplant the parish community. Your school will have Sunday morning services? Yes, okay. Everyone is going to deal with it pastorally different, depending on what is happening. I will tell you how we are dealing with it. We have started a chapel; we have services during the week for the kids. We also have it on the weekend and the people in the community are gathering around and it is becoming a parish. So it has got a double life. It has got a school reality for the kids and then it has a weekend parish. So you have to work, pastorally, on how that is going to balance out. We do not have any other parishes around us, except the monastery, so it is not an issue. If there are parishes, and people are leaving their parishes to attend there, then it needs to be something that the bishop has to regulate.

QUESTION 8:

Concerning languages.

The majority of people who attend our church on Sunday morning are either of a Greek background or Greek speaking. We have a large number of converts (percentage-wise, about a third). Then we have a large number of people who are from a Russian background. It is very Pan-Orthodox. So what I usually try to do is I am working towards the majority of the services being in English. But I do not want to do chanting or services that are not beautiful, or are not appropriate for the Divine Liturgy. So if we cannot chant it in English, for whatever reason, because the translation does not exist, or the chanter cannot really do it, then we do it in Greek. I want to increase that. One of our goals is to start a Byzantine chant school and to train all of our young people to chant in both languages. That is going to take time but ultimately the goal is that we do everything well in English. That is the nature of the Church but it is also the nature of our community there. Most of the people there have English as their first language. The issue of language is very secondary in our community. We do not have this complex where we have to do one or the other. If it is done well, and done with piety, whether they are Greek speakers or English speakers, they love it. Their criteria are right. They want to pray and want something prayerful. It is important to go to English, but it has to be done well and it takes time to do that.

QUESTION 9:

Concerning the position of the non-Orthodox.

You can accept non-Orthodox [in the school] but on the basis they are going to be accepting and that we are not going to change our way of life and we are not going to change our identity. We have a few non-Orthodox in our school. They almost immediately became catechumens. I would accept somebody who is not Orthodox on the basis that they are very open to Orthodoxy and they are going to participate. If they are going to come in with their own agenda or anything, I am not going to accept them into the school.

Let us say they are not catechumens. I would allow them to be present. I probably would never have them pray, like say the prayers. We do not have that anyway. It is very, very limited for the younger children, their prayer is short (at this point). So there is not really an issue. Yet, I think there would be a line drawn, and that would be for their benefit. The line drawn would be for their benefit, because if you start undiscerningly incorporating them into the life of the Church, without the presuppositions of them wanting to be Orthodox, then you are actually undermining their desire and their good uneasiness, and their feeling that they need to become Orthodox. In other words, you are taking away the feeling that they are missing something. It would be very unproductive of us to treat everyone the same, indiscriminately, even in the school setting. There needs to be discernment and discretion.

I know one school in Florida. They have 60% non-Orthodox. It is Russian Orthodox Church Outside Russia. He says they are doing everything. I do not know how he does it. I think it would be very hard to keep the boundaries in that setting (but I would like to see how he does it). Maybe he has some particularly successful way of doing that. Many people have come and become Orthodox in his school. I am not dogmatic on it. It is a question of pastoral discernment, how you are going to deal with each case.

During the Divine Liturgy, the catechumens leave. I am very much in favor of that being reintroduced in the Church. We are in a missionary setting. We are not in the old country, but a missionary setting. We have it in the Divine Liturgy; we should apply it. If we have catechumens they should leave after the prayer for the catechumens. We can do it in a way that does not make them feel, in any way, separate from the rest of the community but as a part of their pedagogical initiation into the life of the Church. I have done that. My father has done that, when he was a priest in Canada, and it has been very successful. People embrace it when you explain to them what it means to be a catechumen and why they need leave after the prayer for the catechumenate. If they are interested and sincere and you are doing your job, they love it. They do not just accept it, they love it. They understand that this is for a time. We are not rejecting you. This is what it means to be in preparation for Baptism and all the rest. So it is a question of doing the work with the people. So when we have the three kids that are catechumens, they leave. They leave the main church. They go into the exonarthex. They are there with someone and usually we keep them busy with something, pedagogically.

QUESTION 10:

Concerning safeguards against error in teaching.

Obviously, we are not going to teach anything we do not believe in. However, in the order of things, in the hierarchy of what is going to remain with the child, he is not going to remember all the lessons, he is going to remember the teacher and the love of the teacher. He is going to take, from that teacher (whether he likes it or not), the methodology, the ethos, the way that they lived, the way that they communicated, the way that they loved the child. That is what is going to remain with him. When you think back to your best teacher, you probably do not remember what they were saying; but you remember their face, their way, some particular moment that you had with them that really remained with you all your life. Obviously, we are not going to become indifferent to what we are teaching. We are going to be very careful that we are teaching the appropriate material, but it is not as important as who we are as teachers and how we are teaching. That is what remains with the people throughout their lives.

The Holy Family of Saint Basil the Great

Archpriest Peter Heers

ABOUT THE AUTHOR

Archpriest Peter Heers is the founder and current head of Uncut Mountain Press (est. 2000), the founder and head of The Orthodox Ethos (est. 2016), and the founder and first editor of *Divine Ascent, A Journal of Orthodox Faith* (est. 1995). Fr. Peter was also the host of the Ancient Faith Ministries podcast, P*ostcards from Greece.*

Fr. Peter is the author of *The Missionary Origins of Modern Ecumenism: Milestones Leading up to 1920*, as well as *The Ecclesiological Renovation of the Second Vatican Council: An Orthodox Examination of Rome's Ecumenical Theology Regarding Baptism and the Church.*

Fr. Peter is also the translator of several books, including *The Life of Elder Paisios* by Elder Isaac (co-translator) and *The Epistles* of Elder Paisios, *The Truth of our Faith* (vols. 1 & 2) by Elder Cleopa and *Apostle to Zaire: The Life of Fr. Cosmas of Grigoriou*, as well as the best-selling children's book *From I-ville to You-ville.*

Fr. Peter was born in Dallas, Texas and raised near San Francisco, California. The son of an Anglican priest, in 1992 his parents and much of his father's parish converted to the Orthodox Church. In 1996 he came to Thessalonica,

Greece, in order to visit Mt. Athos, returning in 1998 to begin the Theological School of the University of Thessalonica. Fr. Peter has undergraduate, master's and doctoral degrees in Dogmatic Theology from the Theological School of the University of Thessalonica, all completed under the tutelage of Professor Demetrios Tselingides.

He lived in the Thessaloniki area for 20 years where he was married to a Thessaloniki native, blessed with 5 children, and ordained to the diaconate and priesthood in 2003, in the Diocese of Kastoria. In 2014 he was made Protopresbyter and Spiritual Father of the Diocese of Ierissou and Agion Oros. He was the rector of the parish of the Holy Prophet Elias in Petrokerasa, a small village in the mountains outside of Thessalonica, from 2006 until 2017.

Fr. Peter served as the instructor of Old and New Testament at Holy Trinity Orthodox Seminary in Jordanville, New York, and later as a Lecturer of Ecclesiology in the Certificate of Theological Studies Program. Fr. Peter was also the Headmaster of Three Hierarchs Academy in Florence, Arizona. He is a regular speaker to parish groups in the United States and Canada. Fr. Peter Heers currently resides outside of Coolidge, AZ.

Archpriest Peter Heers giving the
Commencement Address at Jordanville's 2017 Graduation

UNCUT MOUNTAIN PRESS TITLES

Books by Archpriest Peter Heers

Fr. Peter Heers, *The Ecclesiological Renovation of Vatican II: An Orthodox Examination of Rome's Ecumenical Theology Regarding Baptism and the Church*, 2015

Fr. Peter Heers, *The Missionary Origins of Modern Ecumenism: Milestones Leading up to 1920*, 2007

The Works of our Father Among the Saints, Nikodemos the Hagiorite

Vol. 1: *Exomologetarion: A Manual of Confession*
Vol. 2: *Concerning Frequent Communion of the Immaculate Mysteries of Christ*
Vol. 3: *Confession of Faith*

Other Available Titles

Elder Cleopa of Romania, *The Truth of our Faith*
Elder Cleopa of Romania, *The Truth of our Faith, Vol. II*
Fr. John Romanides, *Patristic Theology: The University Lectures of Fr. John Romanides*
Demetrios Aslanidis and Monk Damascene Grigoriatis, *Apostle to Zaire: The Life and Legacy of Blessed Father Cosmas of Grigoriou*
Protopresbyter Anastasios Gotsopoulos, *On Common Prayer with the Heterodox According to the Canons of the Church*
Robert Spencer, *The Church and the Pope*
G. M. Davis, *Antichrist: The Fulfillment of Globalization*
Athonite Fathers of the 20th Century, Vol. I
St. Gregory Palamas, *Apodictic Treatises on the Procession of the Holy Spirit*
St. Hilarion (Troitsky), *On the Dogma of the Church: An Historical Overview of the Sources of Ecclesiology*
Fr. Alexander Webster and Fr. Peter Heers, Editors, *Let No One Fear Death*
Subdeacon Nektarios Harrison, *Metropolitan Philaret of New York*
Elder George of Grigoriou, *Catholicism in the Light of Orthodoxy*
Archimandrite Ephraim Triandaphillopoulos, *Noetic Prayer as the Basis of Mission and the Struggle Against Heresy*
Dr. Nicholas Baldimtsis, *Life and Witness of St. Iakovos of Evia*
On the Reception of the Heterodox into the Orthodox Church: The Patristic Consensus and Criteria
Patrick (Craig) Truglia, *The Rise and Fall of the Papacy*

St. Raphael of Brooklyn, *In Defense of St. Cyprian*
The Divine Service of the Eighth Œcumenical Council
The Orthodox Patristic Witness Concerning Catholicism
Hieromartyr Seraphim (Svezdinsky), *Homilies on the Divine Liturgy*
Abbe Guettée, *The Papacy*

Select Forthcoming Titles

Cell of the Resurrection, Mount Athos, *The Mystery of Christ: An Athonite Catechism*
Acts of the Eighth Œcumenical Council
Fr. Theodore Zisis, *Kollyvadica*
St. Raphael of Brooklyn, *On the Steadfastness of the Orthodox Church*
George (Pachymeres), *Errors of the Latins*
Fr. George Metallinos, *I Confess One Baptism*, 2nd Edition
St. Maximus the Confessor, *Opuscula: Theological and Polemical Works*
Fr. Peter Heers, *Going Deeper in the Spiritual Life*
Fr. Peter Heers, *On the Body of Christ and Baptism*
Athonite Fathers of the 20th Century, Vol. II

This 1ˢᵗ Edition of

FORMATION IN THE LOVE OF TRUTH

PRINCIPLES OF ORTHODOX EDUCATION

written by Archpriest Peter Heers, typeset in Baskerville, and printed in this two thousand and twenty fourth year of our Lord's Holy Incarnation is one of the many fine titles available from Uncut Mountain Press, translators and publishers of Orthodox Christian theological and spiritual literature. Find the book you are looking for at

u n c u t m o u n t a i n p r e s s . c o m

**GLORY BE TO GOD
FOR ALL THINGS**

AMEN.

www.ingramcontent.com/pod-product-compliance
Lightning Source LLC
Chambersburg PA
CBHW052141070526
44585CB00017B/1922